COMPUTERS FOR SENIORS MADE EASY

Outsmarting Your Grandchildren

By James Bernstein

Bernstein, James
Computers for Seniors Made Easy
Book 26 in the Computers Made Easy series

For more information on reproducing sections of this book or sales of this book,
go to **www.madeeasybookseries.com**

Contents

Introduction.. 7

Chapter 1 – Computer Components.. 8

   Monitors... 8

   Mouse and Keyboard 8

   Speakers 10

   Printers 11

   USB Ports 11

   Digital Cameras 13

   Smartphones 13

   Microphone Headset.. 14

Chapter 2 – Microsoft Windows.. 16

   Logging into Windows.. 16

   Windows Desktop 17

   Windows Start Menu and Taskbar.. 18

   Opening and Closing Programs 20

   Moving and Resizing Windows 24

   Changing the Date and Time.. 26

   Keyboard Shortcuts 27

   Basic Windows File Management 28

   The Windows Recycle Bin 35

   Screen Savers 37

   Changing Your Desktop Background Picture 39

   Changing Your Display Settings to Make Things Larger 41

   Microsoft Store Apps... 43

   Copying and Pasting Text 44

Restarting and Shutting Down Your Computer 46

Chapter 3 – Web Browsers 49

How the Internet Works... 49

Web Browsers and Search Engines 51

Web Browsers 51

Search Engines 54

Tabbed Browsing... 57

Bookmarks\Favorites 61

Website Addresses\URLs 63

Web Browser History 65

Clearing Browser History... 67

Auto Filling Web Forms 69

Microsoft Edge Web Browser 70

Chapter 4 – Using the Internet 74

How to Perform Effective Searches 74

Deciphering Search Results... 79

Saving Pictures and Text from Websites... 89

Finding Directions and Using Online Maps 95

Sharing Websites with Other People 110

Streaming Movies and Music... 111

YouTube and Other Video Sites 112

Online Shopping 118

Popular Shopping Sites... 119

Product Reviews... 134

Secure Payment Methods 140

PayPal 141

Chapter 5 – Online Applications and Services................................. 147

Office Applications 147

Online Banking and Bill Paying.. 154

Online Games 156

Chapter 6 – Social Media 161

Facebook 161

Instagram... 169

Twitter 177

Chapter 7 – Using Email 181

Accessing Your Email... 181

Using Your Email Account 183

Email Folders 185

Attachments 186

Sharing Website Links 187

Chapter 8 – Printers 189

Types of Printers.. 189

Printer Connections... 191

Installing Printers\Scanners 192

Setting Your Default Printer 195

Printer Troubleshooting 196

Chapter 9 – Office Productivity Software.................................... 199

Types of Office Productivity Software.. 199

Microsoft Office Basics.. 203

Chapter 10- Viruses and Spyware 211

    Viruses vs. Spyware 211

    How You Get Viruses and Spyware Infections 211

    Available Software 212

    Manual Scans vs. Scheduled Scans vs. Real Time Protection 213

    Acting on Scan Results 214

Chapter 11 – Staying Safe and Secure Online 215

    Email Scams 215

    Phone Scams 216

    Website Popups 217

    Fake Antivirus Software 218

    File Encryption Scams (Ransomware) 219

    Fake Websites 219

    Secure vs. Unsecure Websites 220

    Providing Personal Information 225

    Browser Toolbars 228

Chapter 12 - Protecting Your Computer 230

    Surge Protectors... 230

    UPS 231

    Cooling... 232

    Theft 232

    Cleaning Your Computer 233

What's Next? 235

About the Author 237

Introduction

These days everyone has a desktop computer, laptop, or at least a device such as a smartphone or a tablet that they use to go online, send emails, watch movies and so on. Technology is a great thing when it works right, but when it doesn't, then we tend to find ourselves cursing at our computers and complaining about how things are too complicated. So, when it comes to technology, the goal is to find a happy medium between the convenience our computers offer and the stress they can cause when they don't do what we want them to do.

Desktop and laptop computers have been around for a long time yet there are still many people that are intimidated by them or are simply not using them to their full potential. If you are going to spend hundreds of dollars on something, it would be nice to get your money's worth!

The goal of this book is to help you find that happy place where you can get the most out of your computer yet deal with the annoyances that can come with owning one. I will cover the basics (in detail) for many topics to better help you understand how things work rather than just telling you to click here or press this key and so on, because knowing *how* something works makes it much easier to understand rather than just clicking away with your mouse. I will also cover some basic troubleshooting topics to try and help you figure out things on your own without having to call the grandkids for help! From time to time I will also add in a little advanced information in case you are curious and want to take things a step further. This book is based on the Microsoft Windows operating system but if you use a Mac, then most of the content will still apply.

So, on that note, let's get things started and turn you into a computer expert—or at least out of the beginner category!

Chapter 1 – Computer Components

Many people who own a computer just see it as a silver or black box that sits on or under their desk with a few flashing lights and buttons on it, but it's what's inside that really counts. The components that make up a computer have pretty much been the same for years but have since received some enhancements in performance (thanks to new technology) that enables computer manufactures to make computers smaller, faster, more energy efficient, and, depending on who you ask, cheaper.

Most computer users don't care what's on the inside of their computer but rather what they have attached to the outside of their computer itself. These devices are referred to as peripherals and there are many different kinds that can be used for many different purposes. In this chapter, I will be going over the basic types that you will find in use with pretty much every computer.

Monitors
Your monitor displays the output of the computer to the screen so you can see what you are doing. There are different types of monitors, but the most commonly used types are LCD and LED, with LED being the newer type of the two. You most likely won't even see any LCD monitors in the store anymore. Monitors come in different sizes and you should choose the size that works the best for your eyes and also your desk!

The best way to shop for a monitor is to go into the store and see one in person rather than take your chances by buying something online. Just keep in mind that the displays will be using some pretty fancy demo videos to make them look as good as they possibly can. And when it comes to size, it's not necessarily the case where a bigger monitor will make things bigger on the screen. Bigger monitors allow for higher resolution, which will mean things like icons and text will be the same size as on smaller monitors, but you will simply be able to fit more on the screen. Of course, you can lower the resolution to make things bigger, but that takes away from image quality, so make sure to weigh all your options.

Mouse and Keyboard
Now obviously you need a mouse and keyboard to use your computer, but you have some options to consider even for these items. All new computers will come with a new mouse and keyboard, but they're usually just good enough to get by with. If you want to upgrade, you can consider going wireless to avoid having extra

cords strung across your desk. One thing you need to consider with going wireless is that you will need to periodically change the batteries in both the mouse and keyboard.

As for the keyboard, some people (including myself) like the bigger style keys that were more popular a few years ago (figure 1.1) compared to the smaller, flatter keys that many people use today which resemble more of a laptop keyboard (figure 1.2). Another thing to consider is if you need a dedicated number pad on the right side of the keyboard, or if using the numbers on the top row is good enough for your needs. Some of the fancier keyboards have buttons that will do things such as run certain programs, adjust the volume, and pause and play your music files, but usually require you to install some additional software to enable that functionality.

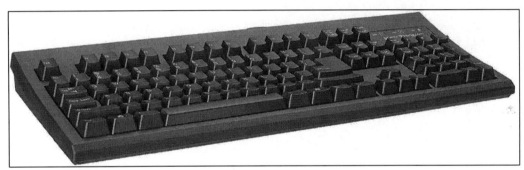

Figure 1.1

Figure 1.2

For the mouse, the most important thing to look for is comfort, otherwise your hand and wrist will be punishing you in no time. Most stores have their mice on display, and this way you can get a feel for which one offers you the most comfort. All mice these days have scroll wheels in between the two mouse buttons (figure 1.3) that allows you to quickly scroll up and down on pages such as documents and websites. Other mice will have additional buttons that are programmable to allow you to assign certain functions to them, but, once again, they will most likely require you to install additional software that should come with the mouse or at least be downloadable.

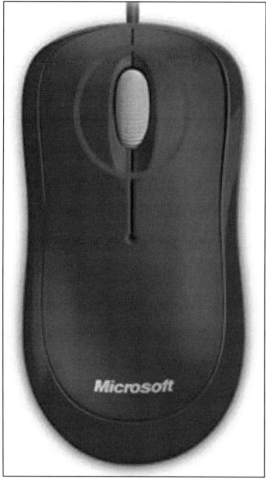

Figure 1.3

Speakers

If you plan on listening to music, playing games, or visiting video sites like YouTube, then you will want a set of speakers to enhance your listening experience. There are a variety of choices when it comes to speakers, ranging from your budget $10 pair all the way to the state of the art 7.1 surround sound multi speaker system that will make you feel like you're at a high-end movie theatre. For most people, a decent pair of speakers with a small subwoofer is sufficient so it doesn't sound like you're at a drive-in movie with the speaker hanging off your window. The speakers will connect to the sound port on the back of your computer, and then to the wall for power, and are pretty much plug and play.

Printers
Another important device you will probably want to get for your computer is a printer. I will have an entire chapter devoted to printers and printing, so I will just mention them for now. There are different types of printers such as inkjet and laser that can perform functions such as faxing, copying, and scanning. Or, if you just need a printer just for the sake of printing, then you can save a few bucks and get a standard printer. If you are the type that likes to print photos rather than just posting them on Facebook, then there are specialty photo printers as well.

USB Ports
Since many of the devices that you connect to your computer will plug into a USB port, I quickly wanted to go over what exactly a USB port is. USB stands for Universal Serial Bus and has had several versions, including 1.1, 2.0, 3.0, and 3.1, with each version becoming considerably faster than the previous version. Computers will typically have around 2-6 USB ports in the rear, and usually a couple in the front of the computer for easy access. As you can see in figure 1.4 these ports are rectangular, and the USB cable can only plug in one way. Many times, the ports will be color coded to tell you which are USB 2.0, and which are USB 3.x and pretty much all new computers come with USB 3.x ports. USB is also backward compatible, meaning you can plug a USB 2.0 device into a USB 3.0 port. There are many devices that use USB connections, and it should remain the standard for years to come.

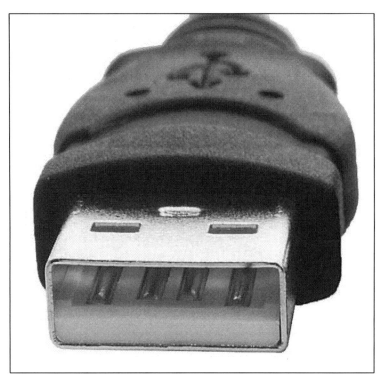

Figure 1.4

Figure 1.5

Be on the lookout for what they call USB C cables. This are a newer version of USB and consists of a smaller connector that can be inserted either direction into the port. They are commonly used for smartphones and on high end laptops.

Digital Cameras

One device that is losing popularity thanks to smartphones is digital cameras. These types of cameras don't use film but rather use memory cards to store the pictures, which allows you to transfer them to your computer or send them off to be printed like you used to do with camera film. Professional photographers still use real cameras and not their phones to take pictures, of course, but some old school people still like their digital cameras and use them to capture special moments rather than relying on their phones. With smartphones coming with better and better cameras, you can expect digital camera sales to drop even more.

Smartphones

Speaking of smartphones, that is next on the list of computer peripherals, even though they are more of a standalone device or can even be considered a computer themselves. Even so, people connect their smartphones to their computers via a USB cable to transfer pictures and movies off of their phones and onto their computers. You can also charge your phone while it's connected to your computer through the USB cable, but it typically won't charge as fast as if you used your wall charger since most wall chargers are "fast" chargers.

There are different makes and models of smartphones, but as of now it's basically a choice of using an *Apple iPhone* or a *Google Android* based smartphone. There are many manufacturers who make Android based phones, and they often customize the interface the way they like so one manufacturer's phone most likely will look and behave a little differently than another's. iPhones look and feel the same between models, but Apple adds more features as the newer models come out.

Depending on what model of phone you have, when you connect your smartphone to your computer a few different things might happen. If it's the first time you have connected it to your computer, it may take your computer a while to recognize your phone for the first time. Then you may or may not get a window that pops up showing the folders contained in your phone's internal storage. Some Android phones, for example, make you pull down from the top notification area menu that has connectivity options such as *transfer files* or to *charge the phone only*. iPhones will typically pop up a message asking if you want to trust this computer, and you have to confirm before it will let you access the phone's storage from your computer. Once you get into the phone's storage, you will typically want to look for a folder that is called *DCIM*, which will have your pictures and video files stored in it. Once you open this folder, you can drag and drop the files onto the desktop of your computer or into another folder of your liking. From there you can print them out, email them, upload them for professional printing, or copy them to a flash drive or external drive to access from a different computer.

If you are an Android smartphone user and would like to learn how to get the most out of your phone without getting confused in the process, then check out my book **Android Smartphones Made Easy**.
https://www.amazon.com/dp/1086026837

Microphone Headset

A microphone comes in handy if you are doing things like video calls using software such as Skype or doing video meetings using software such as Zoom. It can also come in handy for online video gaming where you talk to other players during a battle or race. Or, if you are one that likes to do dictation and uses voice to text software, then a microphone is a must. These microphones connect to your computer using the microphone input jack next to where your speakers connect, or they can also be connected via a USB port. Once you connect the microphone and your computer recognizes it, then you can adjust some of the input levels such as volume from within your recording software or meeting app.

Figure 1.6

As you can see, there are many peripherals you can use with your computer that allow you to expand its capabilities, so it's just a matter of figuring out what you need, finding the device that is best for you, and, most importantly, is in your price range!

Chapter 2 – Microsoft Windows

Now that I have covered the most common components that you need to have to be able to use your computer, I will shift to the software side of things, which is equally important. A computer without software is just an expensive paperweight. There are two main types of software used on a computer that you need to know about. The software that comes installed on your computer to make it run is called the *operating system*. There is more than one type of operating system out there, but I will be focusing on the most popular one by far, and that is Microsoft Windows. Another very common operating system is the Mac OS which is what Apple Macintosh computers run.

In this chapter, I will discuss the major components of Windows, and hopefully by the end of the section you will have a much better understanding of how to use and find the Windows features I discussed. Feel free to play along and try things out on your computer itself as I go over them.

Before I get into Windows, I just wanted to mention the other type of software besides operating systems. Actually, there are multiple software programs or apps that you can install on your computer such as Microsoft Word, photo editing software, email software and so on. This type of software is installed "into" your operating system so if you don't have an operating system to begin with, you can't install any other type of software on your computer.

You will hear the term, software, programs, applications and apps and they all refer to pretty much the same thing. The term apps is more commonly used with smartphones and tablets while software and programs are commonly used with computers even though your computer can run apps. Yes it is confusing and a little overkill!

Logging into Windows

Okay, so you have your new computer in front of you powered up and ready to go. So, what's first? Learning the basics of how Windows operates is essential if you want to be a proficient computer user and not be looking for assistance for things that should be easy to do.

The first thing you will notice every time you turn on your computer is a login screen that requires a name and password. Windows should automatically show your username and you will just need to type in your password or PIN depending on how your computer is set up to log in. Figure 2.1 shows an example of the Windows login screen but rather than the username of Administrator, it would have the username that is configured on your computer. If you bought your computer preconfigured from the store it might have a username of Owner or something similar unless you added your name during the initial setup of the computer.

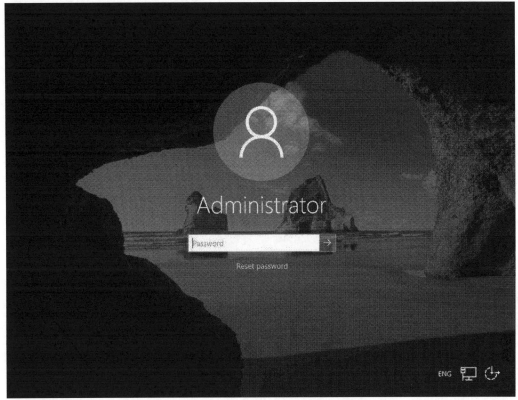

Figure 2.1

If you have more than one user account on your computer then you would be able to select which one you wanted to log in with, but most home users only use one.

Windows Desktop
Once you log into your computer you will be taken to what is called the *desktop*. The word desktop is kind of a vague term that people use in different ways, but essentially the desktop when it comes to Windows is the main screen where you will have icons for programs and other items like folders and files that you

regularly use. Think of it as the top of your desk that your monitor sits on top of. It's where you have an overview of everything and the place where you find the things you need to do your work. Here is what a typical Windows desktop looks like. Notice the icons for programs and the other files and folders as well as the desktop background image? The desktop is customizable, and you can add whatever shortcuts to programs that you like, as well as create files and folders of any type on it.

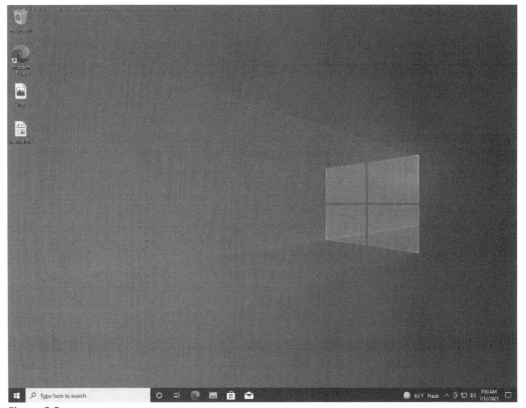

Figure 2.2

Windows Start Menu and Taskbar

At the bottom of the desktop, you might have noticed a bar with some additional icons on it. This is called the *Windows Taskbar*, and its purpose is to house the Start button which displays the Start menu, any programs you might have open, as well as things like the system tray icons, Cortana search box and the clock. The purpose of the Start button is to bring up all the programs and other utilities installed on your computer. These can be programs that have come with Windows, or software you have installed on your own.

Cortana is a feature built into Windows that is similar to Siri on the Apple iPhone. You can ask her questions about things such as the weather or how to find a certain item on your computer. If you have a microphone connected to your computer then you can even use your voice to ask your question.

Figure 2.3 shows an example of the default Windows 10 Start Menu. As you can see, it shows your programs and apps on the left and then also has some categories on the right with what they call "tiles" that are pretty much icons that you can click on to open that particular app. Yours will look a little different depending on what programs or apps you have installed on your computer.

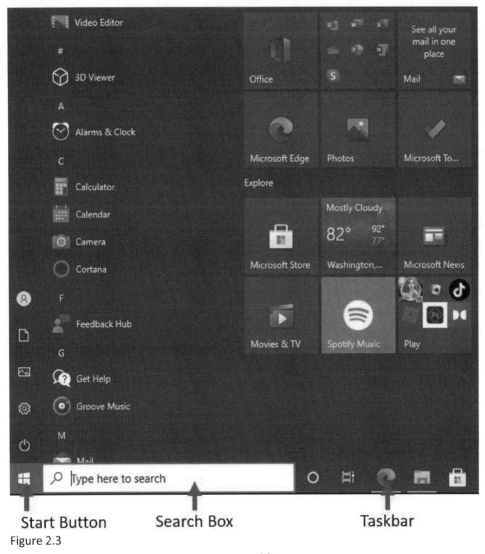

Start Button   Search Box   Taskbar

Figure 2.3

As you open programs on your computer, they will be placed in the taskbar where you can then click on them to bring them to continue working on them. So if you have more than one program open such as a document and also a web page, you can click on the one you want to work on and the other will still be running in the background and you don't need to worry about having to reopen the file or program to continue where you left off.

One thing that can be a little confusing with the taskbar is that it can contain shortcut icons for your programs as well as display programs that you have open. Once you start playing around with opening and closing programs, you will get a better understanding of how things work.

Opening and Closing Programs

Speaking of opening and closing programs, I would now like to discuss how you can open, minimize, maximize and close your programs. In order to use a program such as a word processor or web browser, you first need to open the program. There are several ways to do this and whichever way works best for you is perfectly fine.

You can see your installed programs by clicking on the Start button and then scrolling through the listing of installed programs and apps as seen in figure 2.4. Your available programs and apps will most likely look different than my example.

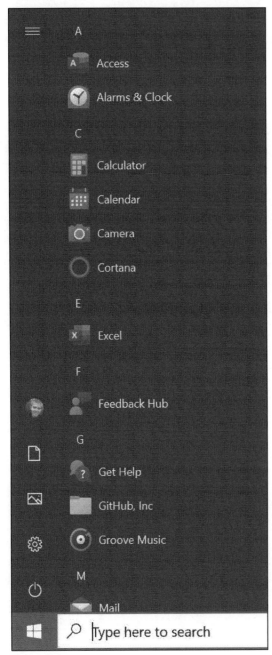

Figure 2.4

You can also click on any program icons you might have on your desktop since many programs will place an icon there when they are installed. You can even add program icons to your desktop as needed so you can have all of your most commonly used programs accessible from one place.

If you are having trouble finding a program's icon to start the program, you can do a search for it in the search box in the taskbar. You will just need to know the name of the program or app you are wanting to open.

Once you have a program open, you can take three main actions on that program about its status. You can minimize it so it's out of sight down in the taskbar yet still open. You can maximize it so it takes up the entire screen rather than just being displayed in what is called a window. Or you can close the program altogether so it's not running anymore.

Let's say I decided to open the calculator app from the Start Menu. Now that's it's open I can see that I have my three main action choices at the top right of the calculator window. If I click on the minimize icon, it will minimize the app down to the taskbar yet still keep it running and I can then bring it back up on the screen when I am ready to use it again. If I click on the maximize icon, it will make the calculator take up the entire screen which would be a little too much for this type of app. If I click the close icon, then it will close the calculator app and anything I was working on will be gone since there is no save option with the calculator.

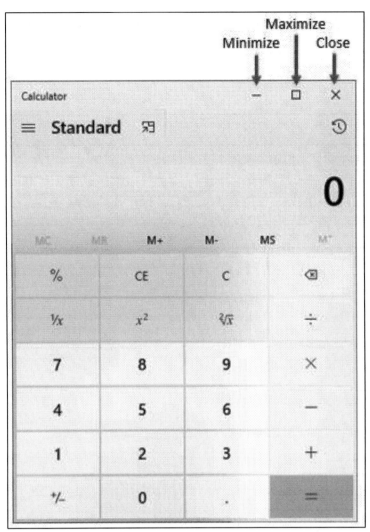

Figure 2.5

One thing I wanted to mention in regards to maximizing your programs and apps is that when you click on the maximize icon, it will then change to a double box icon that you can then click on to have it put back to its original non full screen size.

Figure 2.6

Moving and Resizing Windows

When you have a program open, it's known to be open in a window. You might have put the pieces together with Microsoft Windows since that's technically what the name means.

Once you have your window open, you can then resize it to better suit your needs or move it to a different area on your screen. To resize a window, you will need to first make sure that it is not fully maximized (full screen). Then all you need to do is place your mouse on the side you wish to enlarge or shrink so it makes a double-headed arrow (figure 2.7) and then click, hold and drag the window to set it to a new larger or smaller size.

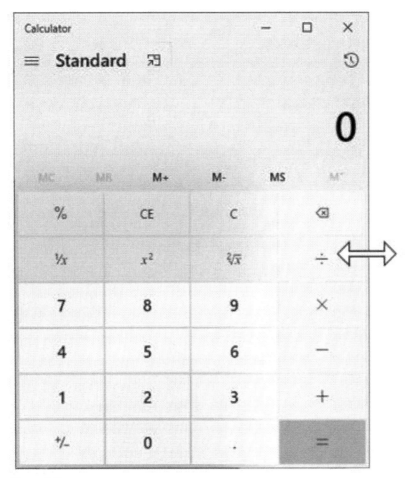

Figure 2.7

Figure 2.8 shows the calculator app after I enlarged it by dragging it from the side to "stretch" it out.

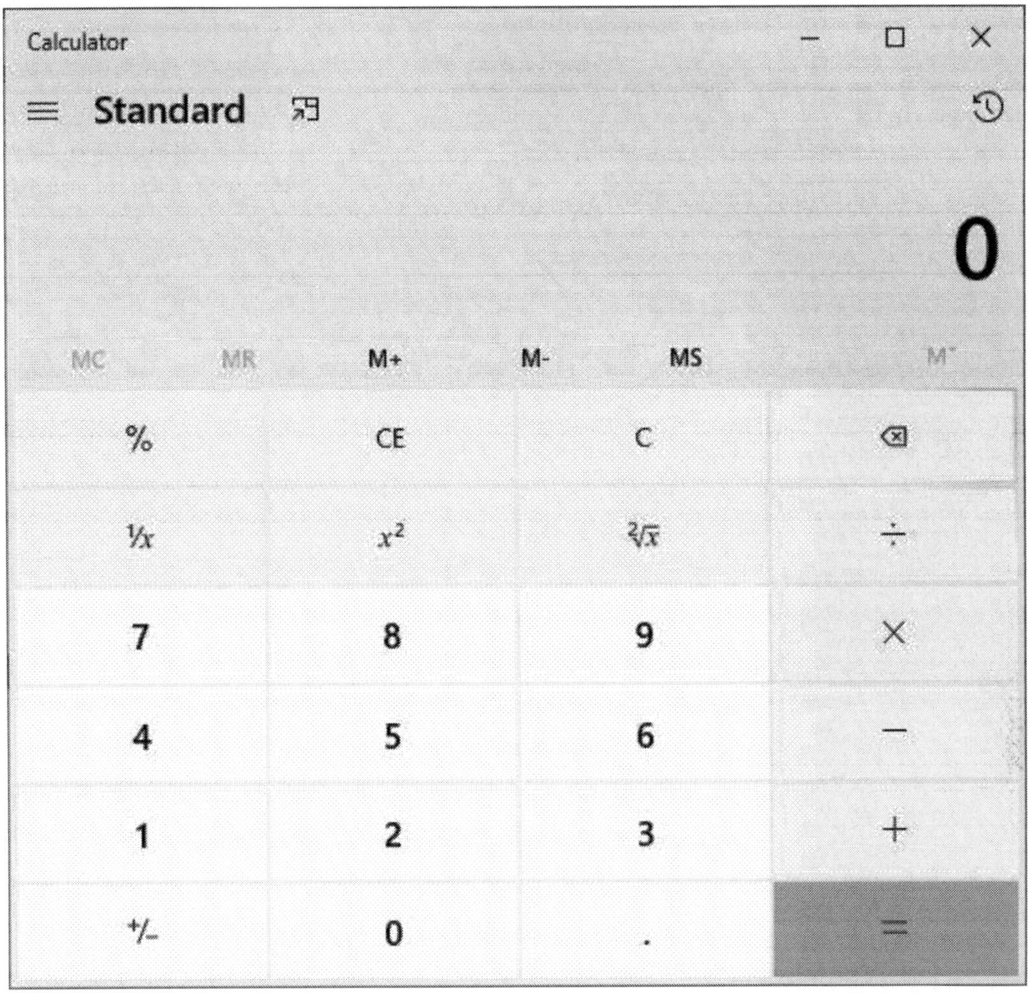

Figure 2.8

To move a window to a different location on your screen you will once again need to make sure it is not fully maximized since that takes up the entire screen and there is nowhere to go!

Then you can click anywhere within the program's title bar as shown in figure 2.9 and hold down your mouse button and drag the window to its new location on the screen and then release the button.

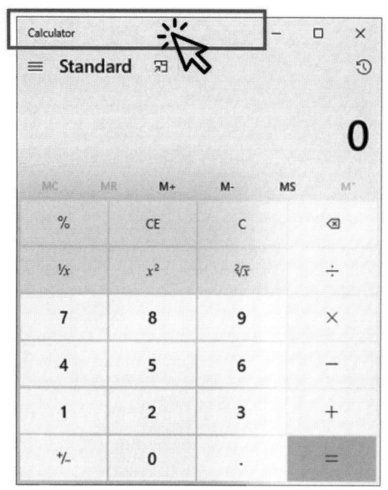

Figure 2.9

Changing the Date and Time

Another thing I will mention in regard to the Taskbar since it's *on* the Taskbar, is how to adjust the date and time settings if needed. Sometimes when you get a new computer or have a new installation of Windows, your date and time settings may be incorrect. This may be because of the incorrect time zone being set, or if your computer's internal clock is off and needs to be adjusted. If it's a case of an adjustment needed with the internal clock, then you may have someone go in and fix it, because every time you reboot your computer it might revert back to that incorrect time.

If it's just a case of setting the correct time zone or Windows itself is off, then all you need to do to fix it is to right click on the clock on the lower right-hand corner of the taskbar and choose *Adjust date/time*. In figure 2.10, you can see that there is a drop-down menu for the time zone as well as some other options. If the *change date and time* button is greyed out, that is because the *set time automatically* option is turned on, so if you want to manually assign the date and time simply turn off this option, and then you will be able to click on the *Change* button. As you can see, there is also a setting for automatic daylight settings adjustments that you can turn on or off as needed.

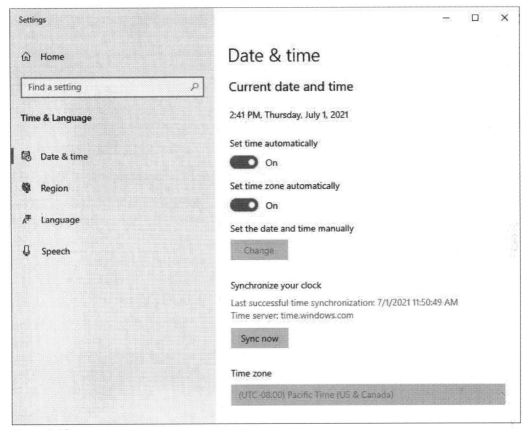

Figure 2.10

Keyboard Shortcuts

Although I talked about the keyboard in Chapter 1, I figure now is a good time to discuss keyboard shortcuts. A keyboard shortcut is a way of pressing a certain key combination on your keyboard to perform the same task you can do by clicking through some menus or clicking on certain buttons with your mouse. If you work with a computer on a regular basis, then you might even know some of them without even realizing it, such as *Ctrl-C* for copy and *Ctrl-V* for paste, which are probably the most commonly used keyboard shortcuts. To use the copy keyboard shortcut for example you would first hold down the Ctrl key on your keyboard and while you are keeping this key pressed you would then press the letter C key on your keyboard. Pressing them individually will not give you the desired result and they need to be pressed using this method.

The good thing about Windows keyboard shortcuts is that they are universal for all Windows programs for the most part, so you don't need to learn specific shortcuts for each program unless that program has its own custom shortcuts built-in. Here is a listing of some of the more commonly used keyboard shortcuts within Windows:

- **CTRL+C** - Copy a file or text.
- **CTRL+X** - Cut a file or text (for moving).
- **CTRL+V** - Paste a file or text.
- **CTRL+Z** - Undo the last operation.
- **CTRL+F** – Find or search for a file or text.
- **CTRL+A** - Select All (text in a document or files in a folder).
- **CTRL+P** – Print
- **CTRL+S** – Save
- **CTRL+O** – Open a file from within a program.
- **SHIFT+DELETE** - Delete selected item(s) permanently without placing the item in the Recycle Bin.
- **ALT+F4** - Close the active item or quit the active program.
- **ALT+ENTER** - Displays the properties of the selected object.
- **ALT+TAB** - Switch between open items.
- **ALT+ESC** - Cycle through items in the order they were opened.
- **CTRL+ESC** - Display the Start menu (The Windows key does the same).

Basic Windows File Management
One of the most important things to know how to do when it comes to Windows, or even any operating system, is knowing how to manage your files and folders. Once you get this figured out, you will notice that using a computer is much easier because knowing how the Windows file structure works will make you much more efficient when using pretty much any program you have on your computer. This is a much more advanced topic so if it's not something you are interested in then you can skip ahead.

Files are items such as pictures, videos, documents and so on, and they are stored in virtual folders to keep things organized. For example, if you have a bunch of photos from your vacation to the Bahamas and want to keep them all in one place, you can make a folder called *Bahamas Vacation* for example, and keep them all in there.

Windows uses a tree structure for its folders with files and\or subfolders within folders. As you can see, there is a folder tree in the left pane with the contents of the Users folder displayed underneath it, and as well as in the right pane (figure 2.11).

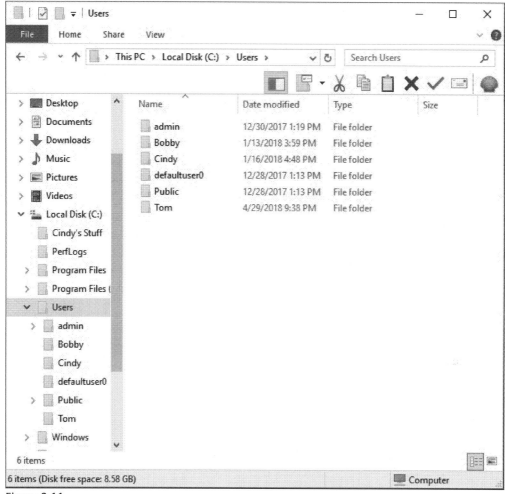

Figure 2.11

To access your files and folders you can use *File Explorer* which is also known as *Windows Explorer*. The easiest way to open this app is to right click on the Start button and choose *Windows Explorer* or *File Explorer* and you will see a window similar to figure 2.11. Within this window, there is the left pane which will show all your installed drives such as your hard drive(s), DVD drive, and any USB connected flash drives or hard drives. Each drive is assigned a letter with the

Windows\system drive assigned the letter C by default. The name of your C drive will vary depending on what the drive label was named during its initial configuration. When you click on a folder in the left pane, the contents of that folder will be displayed in the right pane. You can drill down into these folders and subfolders to see their contents. On the top address bar, you will see the path to the current folder that is highlighted. In figure 2.11 the path is *C:\users*. If you were to drill down to the admin folder the path would then be *C:\Users\admin* and so on.

Changing File and Folder Views

If you don't find the files and folders easy to work with then you can change their view to another format, such as details, list, tiles, large icons, small icons, and so on. To do so, go to the *View* tab and choose the view that best suits your needs (figure 2.12). You can try out different views until you find the one you like best. If you use the details view, then you can sort the files or folders by name, date, size, type, and other attributes.

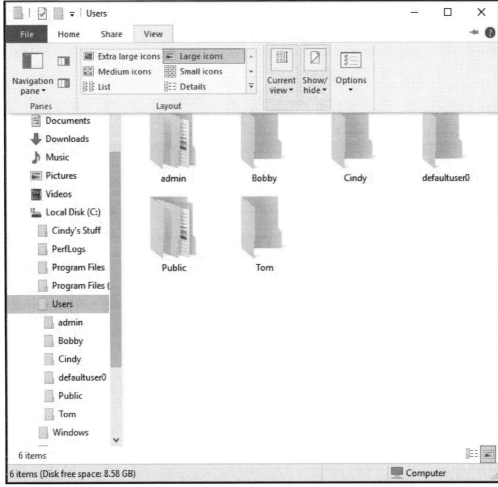

Figure 2.12

Many people like to use the *Large Icons* view for their photos so they can see a preview of all of them within the folder without having to open each of them one at a time to find what they are looking for.

Creating a New Folder
As you save files on your computer you will need a place to store them, and that place is called a folder. There are default folders within Windows used to store documents and pictures etc., but sometimes you will want to create your own folder for a specific purpose such as a place to keep your Bahamas vacation photos. This process is easy to do, and here is how you do it.

To create a folder, you will need to open the Windows\File Explorer by right clicking on the Start Button and choosing Windows Explorer or File Explorer. Then you will need to find the location where you want to create your new folder. Next, you will find a blank spot within that folder, right click there, choose *New* on the drop-down menu, and then *Folder*. Then type a name for the new folder and press Enter. Another method is to go to the *Home* tab in the toolbar (figure 2.13) and click on the *New folder* button.

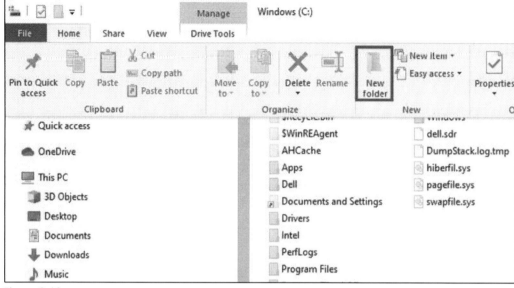

Figure 2.13

When you create your new folder, it will be named *New folder* by default and the text will be highlighted in blue meaning you can either delete the text by pressing the delete key on your keyboard or you can start typing a new name for the folder and it will overwrite the default name.

Figure 2.14

Figure 2.15

Deleting Files and Folders

Just because you have some files such as pictures or documents on your computer, it doesn't mean they are permanent and need to be there forever. If you downloaded some pictures from your phone that you don't like for example, it's easy to delete them from your computer in just a few steps.

There are several ways to delete files or folders and whichever way you choose will accomplish the exact same thing. I will show you three ways to delete a file or folder and you can decide which method you like the best. The first thing you need to do is click one time on the file or folder that you wish to delete. It will then appear highlighted telling you that it has been selected. I will click on my Bahamas Vacation Pictures folder to delete it.

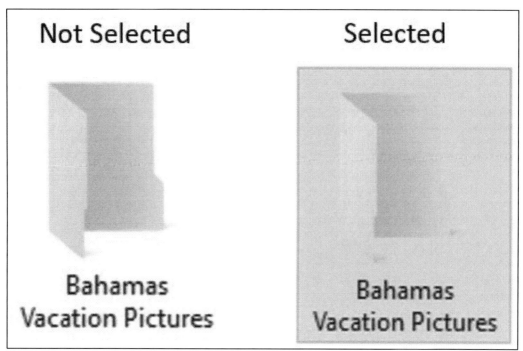

Figure 2.16

When you delete a file, you are just deleting that one file. When you delete a folder, you will also be deleting all of the files stored within that folder. Just like if you were to throw away a file folder with papers inside into your trash can. The file folder and all of the sheets of paper would be trashed.

Now I have a few ways to choose from to delete the folder.

- Press the delete key on my keyboard
- Right click the folder and choose Delete
- Click on the red X in the toolbar from the Home tab (figure 2.17)

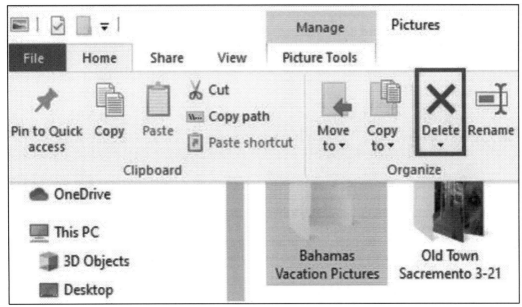

Figure 2.17

The Windows Recycle Bin

Now that you know how to delete files and folders, you might be wondering what happens if you delete something on accident or change your mind after deleting a file or folder?

Fortunately, when you delete a file or folder, it is not permanently deleted but rather sent to the Recycle Bin which can be thought of as your recycle can that you use at home. And just like you can do at home, if you want something back, all you need to do is go over to it and dig it out!

The Recycle Bin can be found on your desktop and looks like a picture of a trash can. The icon will look one way when the Recycle Bin is empty and another way when there are files and/or folders in it.

Figure 2.18

You can open the Recycle Bin by double clicking on it to see what files and folders you have deleted from your computer. You can also see things such as when they were deleted and where you deleted them from.

Name	Original Location	Date Deleted
Bahamas Vacation Pictures	D:\Pictures	7/2/2021 10:41 AM
rs=w_400,h_400.png	C:\Users\Jim\Desktop	6/30/2021 2:04 PM
Windows 11 thumb.jpg	C:\Users\Jim\Desktop	6/27/2021 7:37 PM
tpm thumb.png	C:\Users\Jim\Desktop	6/26/2021 12:51 PM
tpm.jpg	C:\Users\Jim\Desktop	6/26/2021 12:51 PM
Phone	C:\Users\Jim\Desktop	6/24/2021 9:34 AM
Border.jpg	C:\Users\Jim\Desktop	6/24/2021 6:46 PM

Figure 2.19

If you need to restore a file or folder from the Recycle Bin you can simply right click on it and choose *Restore* and it will be placed back in its original location as if it were never deleted.

If you want to permanently delete a file or folder from the Recycle Bin then you can select it and then delete it the same way you did before except this time it will be gone for good. You can also delete everything from the Recycle Bin in one shot by right clicking on it and choosing *Empty Recycle Bin*.

Screen Savers

I'm not sure how many people really use screen savers anymore, but there is still an option to add one in Windows. And the interface you use to do so is the same one that has been around for many generations of Windows.

You can get to the screen saver settings from the *Lock screen* section in the *Personalization* settings which you can get to by right clicking on any blank area of your desktop and choosing *Personalize*.

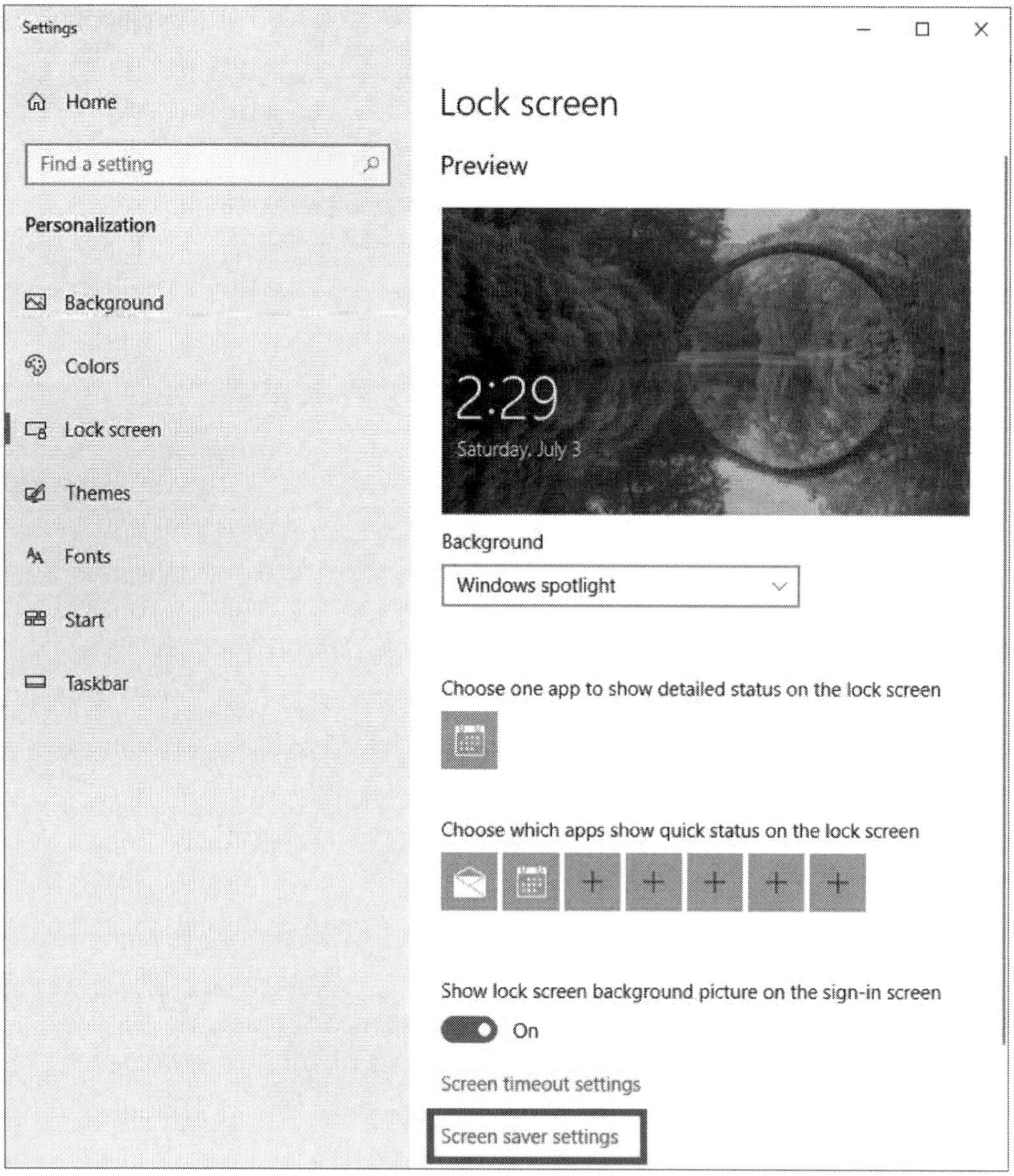
Settings
Home
Find a setting
Personalization
Background
Colors
Lock screen
Themes
Fonts
Start
Taskbar
Lock screen
Preview
2:29
Saturday, July 3
Background
Windows spotlight
Choose one app to show detailed status on the lock screen
Choose which apps show quick status on the lock screen
Show lock screen background picture on the sign-in screen
On
Screen timeout settings
Screen saver settings

Figure 2.20

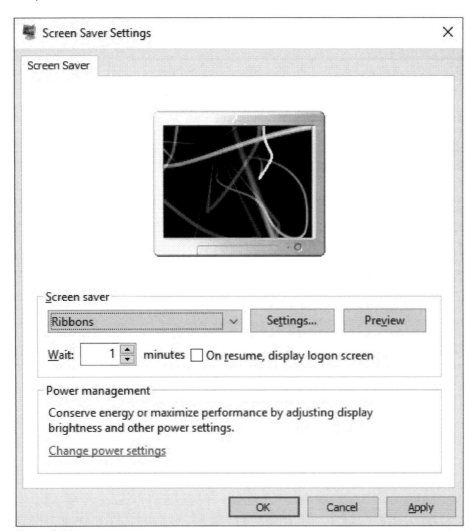

Figure 2.21

Once you have it open, you can choose which screen saver you want to use and how long before it kicks in. This is done by entering a number of minutes in the *Wait* section and when you don't touch your mouse or keyboard for this amount of time, the screen saver will come on. Depending on what screen saver you choose, the Settings button will allow you to customize it to suit your needs. If you want your computer to lock itself after you move the mouse to turn off the screen saver, then click the checkbox next to *On resume, display logon screen*.

Changing Your Desktop Background Picture
One of the most common ways people customize their desktop is to change the background picture of the desktop itself. Windows comes with some high-quality

pictures that you can choose from, or you can use your own pictures or even one you saved from a website.

To change your desktop background, once again right click on a blank area of the desktop and choose *Personalize*. Once you are in the Personalization settings go to the Background section (figure 2.22). Here you will have the option to have your background be either a picture, a solid color, or a slideshow. The slideshow option will change the background image using pictures in a folder that you specify at an interval of your choosing. If you click the *Browse* button, you can browse to a picture stored in a folder on your hard drive to use as a background image. Finally, the *Choose a fit* setting will determine how the picture is displayed on your desktop. You can choose settings such as fill, fit, stretch, tile, and so on.

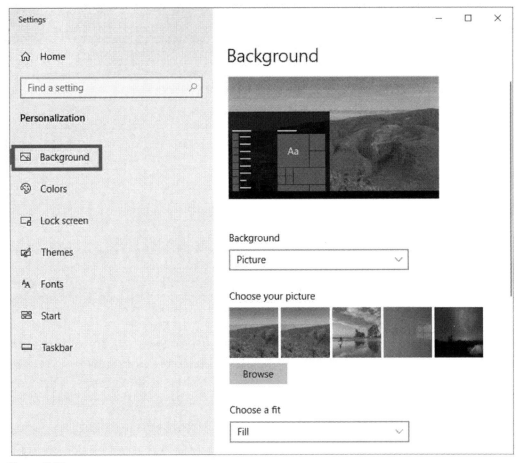

Figure 2.22

 If you are going to use your own picture for your desktop background, try and use a higher resolution (quality) image so it will look nice and clear when it's expanded to fill your desktop, especially if you have a larger monitor.

Changing Your Display Settings to Make Things Larger

Another thing I want to mention that is related to your desktop is the display settings. You can access these settings by right clicking on a blank area of the desktop and choosing *Display settings*, or from the Windows settings under the *System* section (figure 2.23). The Display settings allow you to change the resolution of your computer's display, so you get the best quality image for your monitor size. Windows will normally recommend a setting for you, but you don't have to use it.

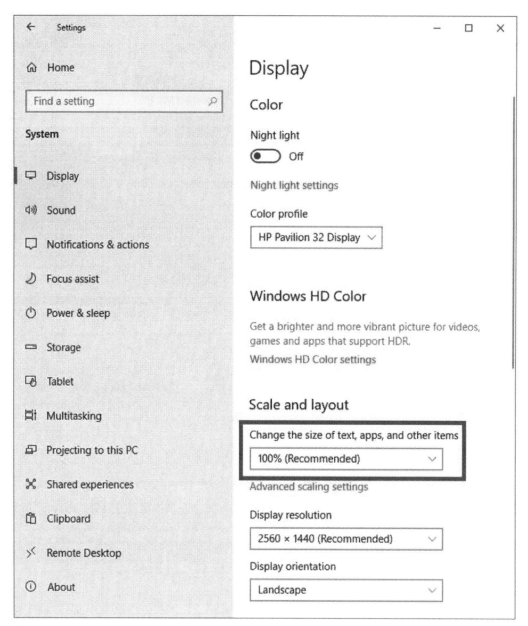

Figure 2.23

The main area here that I want to focus on is the *Scale and layout* section. Here you can increase the things such as the size of text, apps and other items from the default 100% up to 225%. Just keep in mind that this might make some things look better while making other things harder to use because they are too large so play around with this setting until you find the scale that works the best for you.

Microsoft Store Apps

If you have a smartphone, you have most likely used the App Store (Apple) or Google Play (Android) to get more apps for your phone or tablet. Windows comes with the Microsoft Store that lets you search and download new apps that can be used on your computer. There are many free applications to choose from as well as more advanced apps that you can purchase. You can even rent movies and listen to music. So, if you are the type who likes to play games then you are going to want to come here and see what you can find.

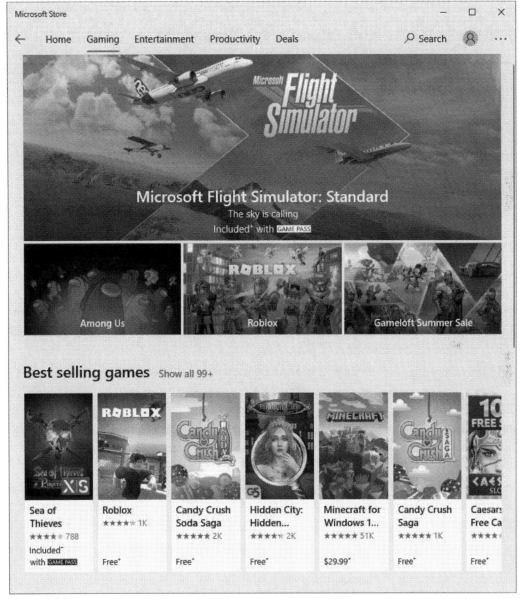

Figure 2.24

To get to the Microsoft Store simply find it on your Start Menu or search for it using the search box by the Start Button. After you find and open the app, you will see a window similar to figure 2.24. As you can see, the Microsoft Store is categorized by types of apps such as games and productivity on the top and then has a search function over to the right.

Once you find an app you want to try out, simply click on the *Get* button to have Windows download and install the app for you. If you scroll down past the *Get* button you will see the system requirements for the app as well as additional information such as the developer's name, release date, and size of the app itself. Just like with your smartphone, there are many apps that you can download and try out for free and many that you can purchase, but just remember that when you install these apps on your computer they will take up disk space, just like regular programs will.

 For now I would stick with the free apps because you probably don't want to enter credit card data into your computer if you can avoid it. Also be sure to read reviews and overall ratings so you don't install something that might not work all that well.

Copying and Pasting Text
One essential skill that every computer user needs to know is how to copy and paste text. Knowing how to do this will make using your computer a lot easier. It will also save you time because you won't have to retype text that you need to duplicate or send to someone else in the form of an email etc.

This process is very similar whether you are copying and pasting text from a web page, Word document, email etc. There is also more than one way to copy and paste text and I will go over the three main methods.

Let's say you have some text with a long and complex code made up of several letters and numbers and you need to send this code to someone in an email but don't want to try and retype it yourself in case you get something wrong.

Make sure you have this code handy for tomorrow. You
need to be sure to have it exactly as shown below.

45845AF57TG244ASL9811EMM

Figure 2.25

To copy the code, all you need to do is select it by clicking on either side of it with your mouse, hold the mouse button down and then drag it to the other side so it becomes highlighted. Now you can use one of the three ways I will now go over to copy the text.

The first method involves using your right mouse button to right click on the highlighted text and then left clicking on the word *Copy*.

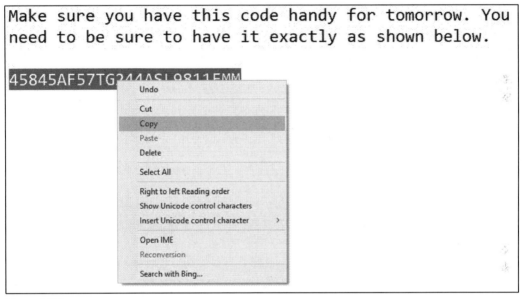

Figure 2.26

You can also use the keyboard shortcut *Ctrl-C* to copy the highlighted text. And finally, if the program that you are copying the text from has a menu item named *Edit*, you can click on that and then choose the Copy selection from there.

When you copy the text, you will not be given any indication by your computer that it has been copied so you just need to assume that it has actually happened.

To paste the text, you will need to go to the program where you want the text to be placed and click in the right location with your mouse. So, if you are pasting it into an email you can start a new email and click in the body of the email where you would like it to be placed.

Then you can right click in that spot and choose *Paste* from the menu or press *Ctrl-V* on your keyboard to use the Paste keyboard shortcut. Finally, you can go to the *Edit* menu in the email program if it has this menu and choose *Paste* from the available options.

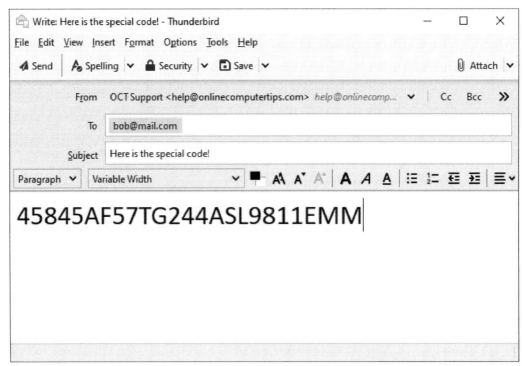

Figure 2.27

Restarting and Shutting Down Your Computer
One thing you are going to need to get used to doing is restarting (rebooting) and shutting down your computer. If you plan on being gone for a long period of time such as on a vacation, you should probably shut it down just in case you have a power outage or if your house will be getting really hot while you are gone.

If you are the type who uses their computer randomly all day, then there is no real reason to shut it off. You might want to just press the power button on the monitor to turn it off if you are going to be away from it for an extended period of time. If you do plan on leaving it on then I recommend restarting it about once a week to keep it running at its best since computers will run better if they are rebooted once in a while. Just make sure you save anything you are working on and close any open programs before rebooting or shutting down your computer.

To restart or shut down your computer, you will need to click on the start button and then on the icon that looks like a power button as seen in figure 2.28.

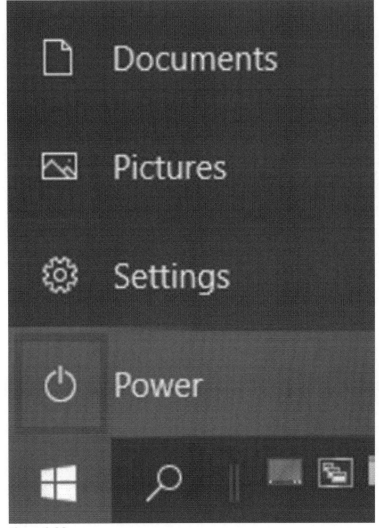

Figure 2.28

Then you will click on the word *Power,* and you will see options for sleep, shut down and restart. Then you would simply click on whichever action you wanted to take.

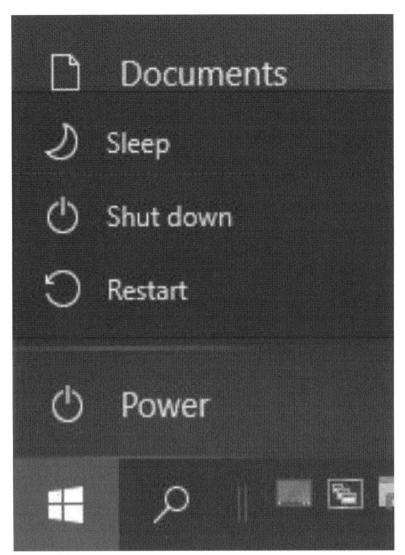

Figure 2.29

Chapter 3 – Web Browsers

When you hear the word *Internet*, what do you think of? Do you think of things like Google, Amazon, and Facebook, or do you think of things like connecting to your computer at the office from your home computer and sharing a spreadsheet with your coworkers via a web browser? Regardless of what you think of, it's most likely that there is much more you can do on the Internet than you think.

Web browsing is just a part of what you can do with the Internet (even though I will be focusing a lot on this part of it since that's most likely what you will be doing on the Internet yourself). However, since it's such a big part of using the Internet, there are things you should know to make the most of it while keeping you and your personal information safe at the same time.

How the Internet Works
The Internet is a very complicated network of computers and networking hardware which I won't be getting into too much detail about, but I think it's a good idea that you know the basics of how it all works. In the next section I will go over some basic networking to hopefully tie it all together. If you don't care about how the Internet works and only care that it works period, then you can skip this section if you want to get to the content that interests you.

The Internet is basically a network of computers (or servers) that are all connected together using connections that are capable of communicating with each other to allow information to pass back and forth through these connections. Back in the beginning these connections were simple, but now they are very complex, and information has to travel through many paths to get where it's going. Just think about if you were visiting a website in another country or continent how far the text and images from that website have to travel to make it to your computer screen and how fast they get there. It's not like there is a cable connecting your computer to the webserver in that country, but rather multiple connections being made to accomplish that task. Figure 3.1 shows the basic idea of your computer at home in the United States connecting to a web server in Europe, and also to one in South America going to two different websites. It's not as simple as the one line between the two shown in the diagram makes it out to be, but rather multiple connections in many locations transferring the data back and forth between the computers.

Figure 3.1

Your computer makes its connection to the webserver by using the public address of that web server. These public addresses are assigned to the companies who are hosting the web servers in their facilities and are unique to them so there is no confusion as to where to send the data.

Then the webserver sends the data you requested (the web page) back to your computer, and you can now view it on your screen. Once that connection between your computer and the webserver is made, it stays connected until it's broken when you do something like close your web browser or turn of your computer etc.

Web Browsers and Search Engines

If you plan on being a regular "web surfer" and utilizing the Internet on a regular basis, then that will require you to use a web browser to do so because without one then you are not going to get too far… if anywhere at all. And if you are going to perform searches on the Internet, then you will need to use a search engine for that. One common mistake many people make is confusing a web browser with a search engine or thinking they are both the same thing when in fact they are not at all.

What's the Difference?

The difference between and web browser and a search engine boils down to that a web browser is software installed on your computer used to display web pages, while a search engine is a website that you use WITHIN a web browser to perform searches. So technically you are using a search engine website to search for other websites by using web browser software.

This may sound a little redundant, but after you read the next sections that go into details about web browsers and search engines, things will make a little more sense. Knowing the difference between the two will make you a more efficient web user and will also allow you to experiment with different browsers and search engines to find the ones that work best for you. And yes, there are more than one of each!

Web Browsers

Like I mentioned in the last section, a web browser is software installed on your computer that is used to display the text and images from websites. Most computers and other devices come with one or more already installed, but you can install others and use more than one at a time. For example, Windows 10 computers will come preinstalled with the Edge web browser and Apple computers (and iPhones) will come preinstalled with the Safari web browser. When reading this information, keep in mind that the process for various tasks will vary between browsers and it's impossible to show every process for every browser. Here is a listing of the more commonly used web browsers:

- Google Chrome
- Microsoft Edge
- Opera
- Safari
- Mozilla Firefox

You can install more than one web browser on your computer so you can try them out and find the one that you like best. For the most part, they all operate in a similar fashion, but they will vary in ways such as how the menu items are laid out, how bookmarks are used, and also how they perform. Plus, they are all customizable to some degree so you can tweak them to your liking.

Figure 3.2 shows an example of the Microsoft Edge web browser that comes installed with Windows. As you can see, there are a lot of components that make up a web browser, but that doesn't mean you should be intimidated by them.

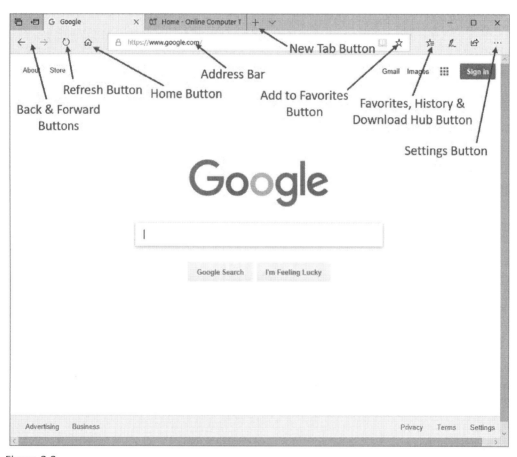

Figure 3.2

Now I will go over each of the main areas of a typical web browser. Keep in mind that they can vary a bit from browser to browser.

- **Address Bar** – This is where you type in the website addresses you want to go to if you prefer to do that rather than do a search for the site. (I will discuss addresses some more later in the chapter.)

- **New Tab Button** – All modern browsers allow you to have multiple website pages open within one web browser session. Simply click the new tab button and it will open up another page that you can use to browse to another site while leaving your other pages open. (I will go into tabs later in this chapter.)

- **Add to Favorites Button** – Use this button to add websites that you are on to your favorites so you can easily find them later and go back to them. Favorites are also known as bookmarks.

- **Home Button** – Clicking on this button will take you to your home page, which can be customized to whatever you want it to be.

- **Refresh Button** – If you want to reload the web page you are on to check for updates or in case it doesn't seem to be responding, you can press this button. (F5 on the keyboard will do the same thing.)

- **Back & Forward Buttons** – You can cycle backward and forwards through all the pages you have been to within a certain tab with these buttons.

- **Favorites, History & Download** – If you go here you can view your favorites or bookmarked sites, go through your browsing history, and also look at your downloaded files.

- **Settings Button** – This is where you can configure and customize your browser to suit your needs. You can also do things like set your default home page, clear your history, and check out your saved passwords.

Now that you can see the main components of a typical web browser, you can try out some other browsers if you have any installed on your computer to see how they work and find the one that works best for you.

 I like to stick with one web browser because once you start having it save things (like your information, bookmarks, and passwords) it will make things more complicated when switching back and forth between other browsers since one will most likely have information stored that another won't.

To install another web browser simply go to the website for that browser, download the installation file, and install it like you would any other program on your computer, or have someone install it for you.

Once you find the browser you want to stick with, then it's a good idea to make it your default browser on your computer or mobile device. How to do that is beyond the scope of this book, so you might want to get some help with the process. The reason you want to do this is because if you click on a link within an email, for example, your computer will use its default web browser to open the website, so you want to make sure it's using the right browser. Another option is to uninstall the browsers you don't want so you only have one. Keep in mind that many operating systems (Windows, Mac etc.) won't let you uninstall their built-in browser.

Search Engines
Now that you have an idea of what a web browser is, I will now go over search engines. A search engine is a service that allows you to search for content on the Internet via a web browser. There are many companies that provide this service free of charge for you to use. The search engine providers "crawl" the web and index its content in their own databases so when you search for a specific word or phrase, it can find the websites that match what you are looking for.

You have most likely heard of Google, and they have the most popular search engine in use today. Providing search engines is not the only thing Google does, of course, but that is how they got their start and is one of the reasons they are such a huge company today. Here is a listing of some of the more popular search engines, and there are many more out there besides the ones in my list:

- Google
- Bing (by Microsoft)
- Yahoo
- Ask

- AOL
- DuckDuckGo

To get to a search engine all you need to do is type its address\URL (discussed later in the chapter) into the address bar of your browser. Or you can even use one search engine to do a search for a different search engine. For example, in figure 3.3 I used the Google search engine to do a search for Bing (the results are shown in figure 3.4). (I will get into more details about how to do web searches in the next chapter).

Figure 3.3

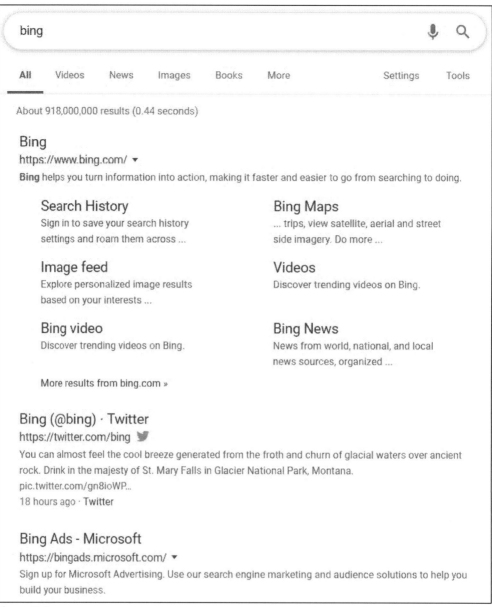

Figure 3.4

Then when I click on the first result for Bing it will take me to **www.bing.com**, where I will then see something similar to figure 3.5. Then I can type in my search criteria in their search box and do my searches from there.

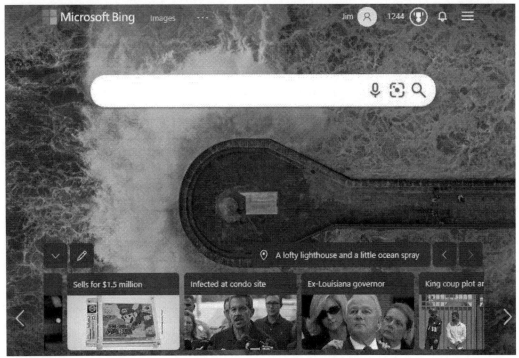

Figure 3.5

When trying out different search engines, you will notice that some like to have other content on the page such as news stories or pictures, while others (like Google) get right to the point and just have a search box.

Using different search engines will yield different results for your searches since they are not all sharing the same information and build their databases and crawl the Internet differently from each other. So, if you are not getting the results you are looking for from one particular search engine, then you might want to try another. (I will go over how to perform effective searches in Chapter 4).

Tabbed Browsing
One of the greatest inventions when it comes to web browsers is the addition of tabs which let you have more than one website open at a time. In the old days, if you wanted to be on two or more websites at a time, you would have to open multiple instances of your web browser. For those of us who have multiple

websites open all day long, that can get messy, but thanks to tabbed browsing, things are a lot more organized and easier.

Figure 3.6 shows the Google Chrome web browser open with a single default tab. You will always have at least one tab open when using any web browser. Since my home page is set to google.com when I open my browser, it automatically goes to their website.

Figure 3.6

Next to that tab is a + sign, which is what I would click on to open up a new tab within my browser. Doing this does not close the existing tab, but rather opens up an additional one next to it (as seen in figure 3.7). Now I have Google open in the first tab, and www.onlinecomputertips.com open in the second tab, and I can go back and forth between them. By the way, most browsers will open your default home page when you click on a new tab.

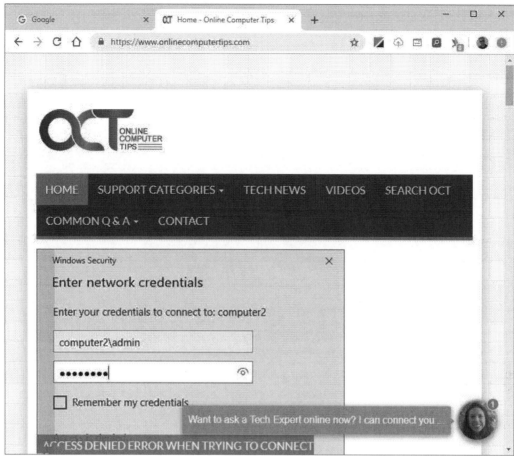

Figure 3.7

As you can see in figure 3.8, you can have as many tabs open as you want and switch back and forth between them. So, if you like to have your email, news, Facebook, YouTube, etc. pages all open at the same time, it's very easy to do.

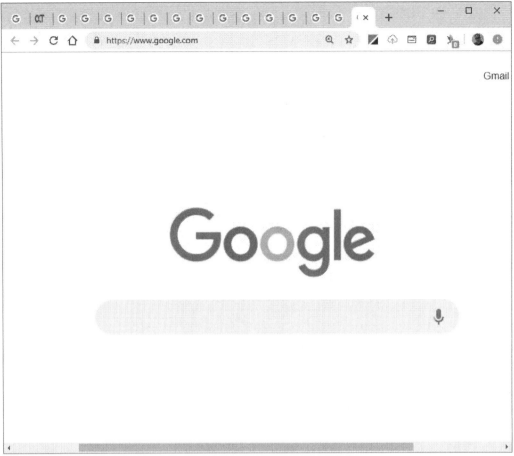

Figure 3.8

If you don't like the order that your tabs are open in, most browsers will let you drag them around to rearrange them however you see fit. And if you want to close a particular tab, simply click on the X on the tab itself and it will leave the others open. If you want to close all of them, then you can either do so one by one or simply close your web browser altogether.

 Many web browsers will allow you to configure them to remember what tabs you had open the next time you launch the browser. So, if you like to have the same ten tabs open every time you start your computer or re-open your web browser, then that is something you can do fairly easily.

Bookmarks\Favorites

Most, if not all, Internet users will have websites that they like to go to on a regular basis. But rather than have to remember what they are or what the website name is, they use bookmarks (or favorites as they are sometimes called) to save these websites in their web browser for easy access. Once you create a bookmark all you need to do is click on it and it will take you to the exact website and section of that website that you were on when you created it.

These bookmarks are created and accessed differently depending on what web browser you are using, but the process is very similar between all of them. For example, figure 3.9 shows how to add the current website page you are visiting to your bookmarks in Google Chrome by clicking on the three vertical dots at the top right of the browser window, and then choosing *Bookmarks* and the *Bookmark this page* option.

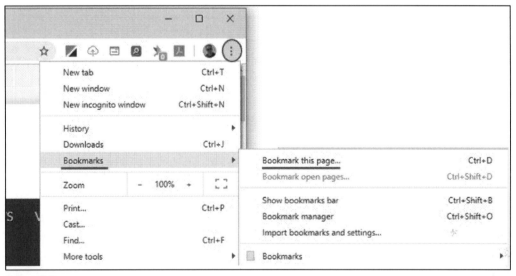

Figure 3.9

When you add a bookmark, you are prompted to give it a name or keep the name that it chooses, which is based on the webpage you are bookmarking. If you have bookmark folders, you can choose to have the bookmark be placed in a specific folder.

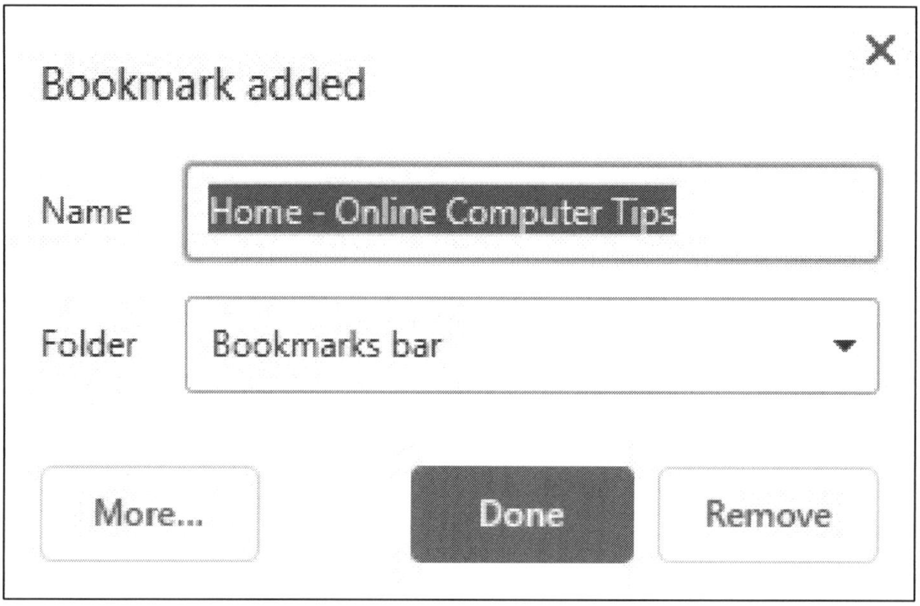

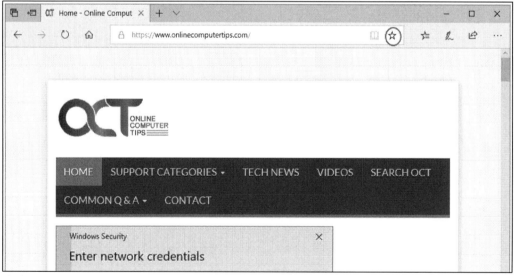

Figure 3.10

Figure 3.11 shows you how to add a favorite in Microsoft Edge by clicking the star icon to the right of the website's address. Remember that bookmarks and favorites are the same thing, and Microsoft is the one who usually refers to them as "favorites" while most other browsers use the term "bookmarks".

Figure 3.11

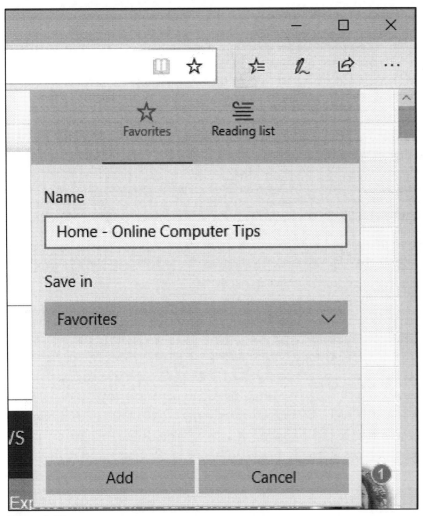

Figure 3.12

Most web browsers will also let you have a bookmark toolbar at the top of the browser where you can have your most commonly used bookmarks listed so you can simply click on the one you want without having to take the extra steps to go to your bookmark menu. There is also a way to edit these bookmarks/favorites if you want to give them a more descriptive name than you did when you first created them.

Website Addresses\URLs
All websites have addresses that are friendly names we use to connect to a web server located somewhere in the world. Without these addresses, your computer wouldn't know where to go to find the information you are looking for. These days

we are bombarded with website addresses in advertisements or TV commercials and so on.

A URL (Uniform Resource Locator) is a fancy name for a website address so if you hear someone saying they need the URL of the website you are on, they mean its address.

Addresses\URLs will show what page you are on within a certain website. So, if you are on a pet store website called **petstore.com** and click on a link for the dog food section you might see the address change from **petstore.com/home** to **petstore.com/dogfood**. You really don't need to worry about things like this, but I just wanted to mention it in case you were interested.

 You might have noticed that some website addresses have **www** in front of them while others don't, but you can still get to that website. This is because the people running the site configured it so if you don't put www in front of the name, it will take you to the same place either way.

To find the address of the website you are on, simply look in the address bar and that will tell you the name of the website you are on. You can also copy and paste this text and email it to someone so they can easily get to the same website on their computer.

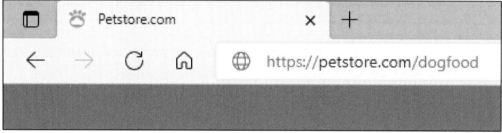

Figure 3.13

You can also highlight the address in the address bar and copy and paste it into another browser, another tab, email, document, or anywhere else you can copy and paste text.

Web Browser History

As you browse the Internet your web browser will keep track of what sites you visited just in case you want to go back to an earlier point in time or a different day and find a site that you went to before. This can come in handy when you forget to bookmark something or your browser doesn't remember your last browsing session after you reopen it, and by that I mean that most web browsers have a feature that will open all the sites and tabs you had open after you close the browsers so you can continue where you left off. This option can usually be turned off if you don't want that feature active.

The amount of history that is kept varies between web browsers and is usually customizable or can sometimes even be turned off. To view your browsing history, find the history option within your particular browser to bring up your history results. Sometimes you can bring up the current day, last week, or even recently closed tabs. Then when you find the site you were looking for you can simply click on it to bring it back up again. Some browsers such as Google Chrome will let you delete individual history items by selecting that site and then clicking on delete (figure 3.14). All browsers will let you delete your entire history, or even let you delete just the current day or previous hour.

Chapter 3 – Web Browsers

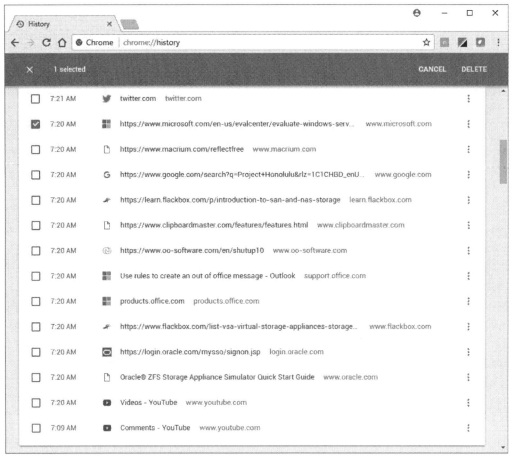

Figure 3.14

66

Clearing Browser History

There may come a time when you want to erase where you have been from your browser while in normal browsing mode. This is where clearing your history comes into play, and it's something you can easily do whenever you like. As you access websites, your computer or mobile device keeps track of where you have been and also does things like keeps images from sites so when you go back to that site it doesn't have to re-download the images from that page and rather just loads the ones on your computer, making that site load faster.

Over time your computer can get cluttered with these images and also other temporary files like cookies that your web browser keeps as you visit websites throughout the day. These files take up space on your hard drive, and over time can even slow things down a little, so clearing your history and temporary files is something you might want to think about doing.

Most browsers will let you choose what type of information and files you can delete and also from what time period. So, let's say you want to remove your browsing history for the past week, but leave the rest. You most likely will have an option to do that. Or let's say you want to delete temporary Internet files but keep your cookies. That should be an option you have as well.

Just like with everything else, how you clear your history will vary depending on what web browser you are using, and I will be using Google Chrome for my example so the process you use might not be the same depending on your browser. To access your history in Chrome simply go to the three vertical dots at the top right and choose *History*.

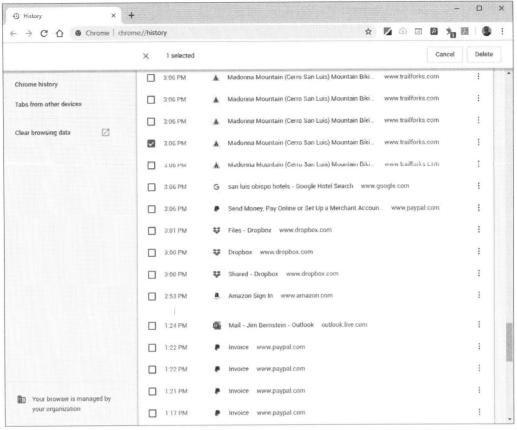

Figure 3.15

Figure 3.15 shows the current history, and you can scroll up and down the list to see where you (or others) have been. If you want to go to the webpage related to a specific history item, all you need to do is click on it. Or, if you want to remove a specific history item, simply check the box next to it and click on the *Delete* button.

If I want to remove my history items in bulk, I can click on *Clear browsing history* and I will see a screen similar to figure 3.16. As you can see, I can choose the time range such as all time, the last hour, the last 7 days, and so on. Then I can choose which history items I want to have removed. Normally you can stick with the defaults and be okay, but if you are planning on really clearing out your browser, you can also have any saved passwords and form information (such as saved addresses) removed as well. If you do clear out your saved passwords and form information, you will manually need to enter the info the next time you go to any websites that you had the information stored for previously.

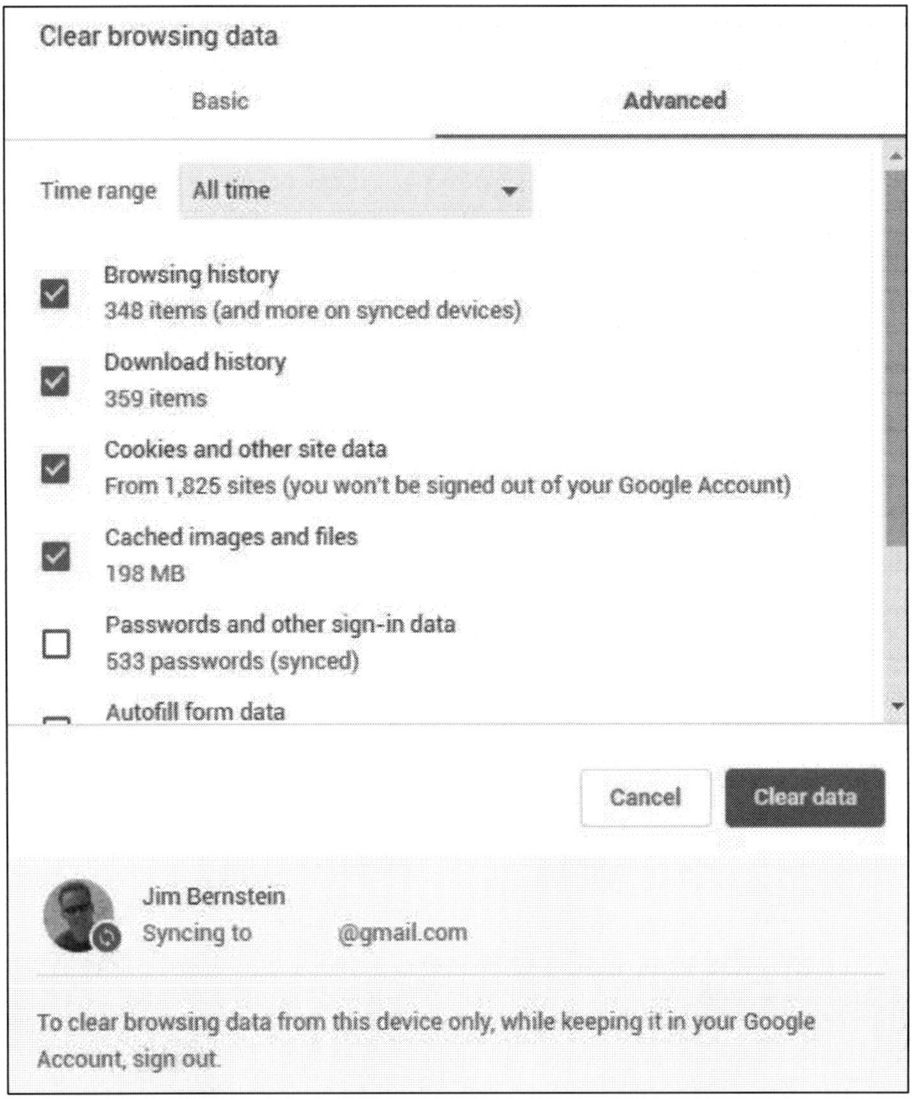

Clear browsing data

Basic	Advanced

Time range   All time   ▼

☑ Browsing history
348 items (and more on synced devices)

☑ Download history
359 items

☑ Cookies and other site data
From 1,825 sites (you won't be signed out of your Google Account)

☑ Cached images and files
198 MB

☐ Passwords and other sign-in data
533 passwords (synced)

☐ Autofill form data

Cancel   Clear data

Jim Bernstein
Syncing to   @gmail.com

To clear browsing data from this device only, while keeping it in your Google
Account, sign out.

Figure 3.16

Auto Filling Web Forms

Web browsers have the capability to remember common information such as your
name, address, phone number, and email address, and can then fill that
information into forms on websites automatically when needed. For example,
let's say you are on a website making a purchase and are at the part where you
need to put in your shipping information. If your browser has saved that
information from a prior time you entered this info, then it can fill in all the fields
for you so you will not have to type them in each time. Most browsers will ask you
if you want to save this type of information and also ask you to save usernames

and passwords for website logins. This feature can be turned on or off within the web browser settings, so it's not mandatory that you use this feature.

Web browsers will usually not let you have them keep stored information for things like credit cards or social security numbers. One thing you should think twice about is having your browser save passwords for sites that can be a security risk, such as banking sites or even your email accounts. If someone can get your Windows password, then they will be able to get all of your saved website passwords from browsers such as Google Chrome and Microsoft Edge etc. If you do have saved passwords in your browser, then you can always go in there and remove them and then the next time your browser asks if you want it to remember your password for a site you can say no.

Microsoft Edge Web Browser
If you are using Windows 10 on your computer which you most likely are, then you will automatically have the web browser called Microsoft Edge installed on your computer. For most people, Edge works perfectly fine for browsing the internet and checking email etc.

The way Edge works is similar to all the other web browsers, and you should definitely try it out and see if you like it. Microsoft claims it's faster than Chrome and Firefox, and also says it's a good browser to use if you are into staying safe on the Internet. And since you can run multiple browsers on your computer at the same time, it never hurts to have a couple that you like since some pages work better in different browsers.

As you can see in figure 3.17, Microsoft Edge looks like your typical web browser, with the address bar at the top, a home button, back and forth buttons, and the ability to open multiple tabs within one browser window.

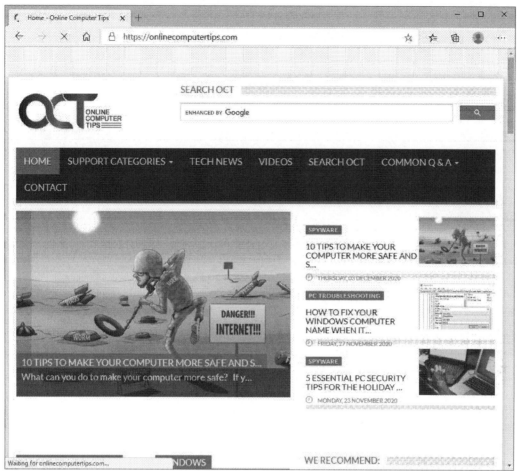

Figure 3.17

If you have ever used a web browser such as Chrome or Firefox, then you shouldn't have too much trouble using Microsoft Edge. It works the same way once you get your home page configured so it has a familiar look when you start it up. There are only a few areas you really need to get familiar with before you will be up and running (figure 3.18). I showed you a similar graphic of the Edge browser earlier in the chapter, but it doesn't hurt to have a refresher! Below you will see the main components of Edge and a summary of what they do. Keep in mind that you only need to remember the features that you will be using!

Figure 3.18

- **Address Bar** – This is where you type the website addresses you want to go to if you prefer to do that rather than do a search for the site.

- **New Tab Button** – All modern browsers allow you to have multiple website pages open within one web browser session. Simply click the new tab button and it will open up another page that you can use to browse to another site while leaving your other pages open.

- **Add to Favorites Button** – Use this button to add websites that you are on to your favorites so you can easily find them later and go back to them.

- **View Favorites** – If you go here you can view your favorites or bookmarked sites, as well as organize them into folders etc.

- **Home Button** – Clicking on this button will take you to your home page, which can be customized to whatever you want it to be.

- **Refresh Button** – If you want to reload the web page you are on to check for updates or in case it doesn't seem to be responding, you can press this button. (F5 on the keyboard will do the same thing.)

- **Back & Forward Buttons** – You can cycle backward and forwards through all the pages you have been to within a certain tab with these buttons.

- **Collections** – This feature can be used to save web information such as images, text or entire pages into one place so you can retain this information and refer back to it later.

- **Personal Info** – You don't need to log into your Microsoft account in order to use Edge but if you are logged in then you can view and manage your profile settings from here.

- **Settings Button** – This is where you can configure and customize Edge to suit your needs.

So now that you know what all the important buttons do, you can start browsing and searching to find exactly what you're looking for.

Chapter 4 – Using the Internet

Now that you have a better understating of the more technical side of web browsers and search engines, it is time to start seeing what kind of cool stuff we can find out on the Internet. Speaking of cool, the phrase "surfing the Internet" is kind of outdated, so if you want to look cool in front of others, you might want to avoid using it. (I still like it though!)

How to Perform Effective Searches

There is more to searching the Internet than just putting in a word or phrase and pressing enter to see your results. Sure, it will work fine for the most part, but there are other methods you can use to get more accurate results. On the other hand, if you can find what you need with simple searches then that's ok too, since most of the time that is what I do as well. Some of this information is a little on the advanced side so don't feel bad if it all doesn't make sense!

When typing in a word or phrase into a search engine, it will search for all of those words no matter what order you type them in. So, if you type in **top rated dog food**, your results will be pretty much the same as if you typed in **dog rated food top,** as you can see in figures 4.1 and 4.2.

Figure 4.1

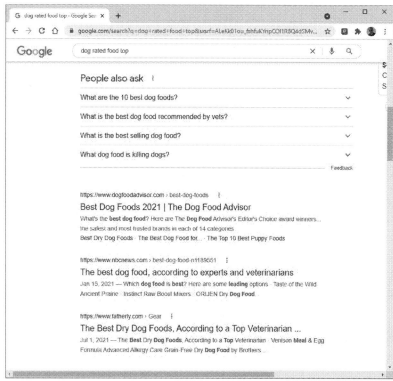

Figure 4.2

You want to be as specific as you can to avoid getting irrelevant results or too many results that you will have to sift through to find what you need. Many times you can even do your search in the form of a question, such as *what is the best computer for gaming* or *how do I make chicken alfredo* because it might be a commonly asked question or search term.

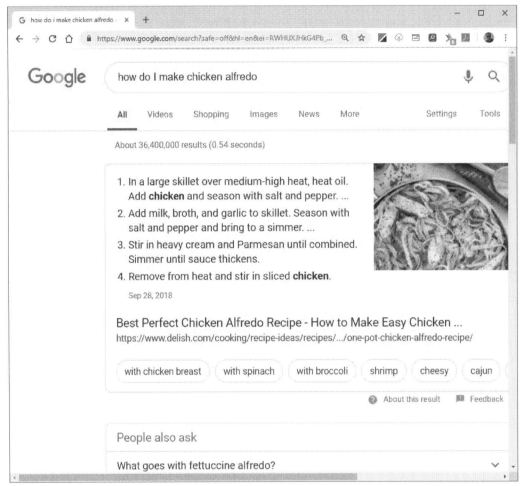

Figure 4.3

There are many tricks you can use to improve your search results, and I will now go over some of the more useful ones which you can then try out and see how they work for you.

Stay away from common words
Google (and other search engines) ignores most common words and characters such as "and" and "to", as well as certain single letters and digits because they tend to slow down your search without improving the search results. So try and

design your searches to use more unique words that will give you less generic and unrelated results.

Use quotation marks for phrases

If you put quotes around your search phrase, then Google will find results that contain all of the words in the exact order you have entered them in the search box. For example, if you wanted to look up pages on George Washington but didn't want to get results containing other people named George or results about Washington State or Washington DC, you could type in "George Washington" and Google will find pages with that exact phrase in it. You do not need to worry about capitalization either. You can also use this for longer phrases such as "blue 1969 Camaro z28" if you wanted to get specific. Notice in figure 4.4 how Google found images matching blue 1969 Camaro z28, and also the exact phrase, which it highlighted in bold within the search results.

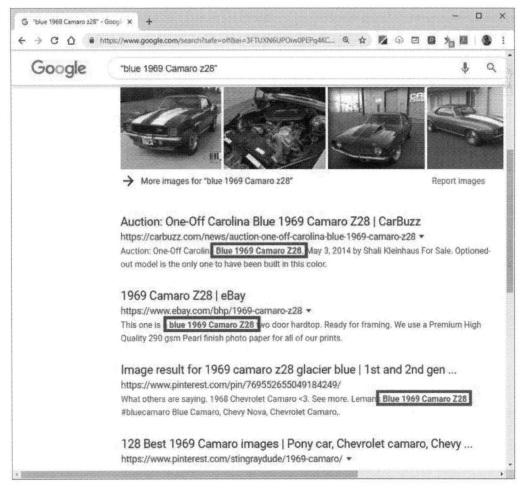

Figure 4.4

Using the "+" search variable
If you are looking for a certain thing on the Internet but need to include a specific word in your search results, then you can use the plus sign to have your browser include your keyword in its results. For example, if you were looking up pickup trucks and wanted to include Ford brand trucks in your search, you can type in **pickup trucks + ford** in the search box. Just make sure you put a space before the +.

*Using **OR** to find two results*
To find pages that include either of two search terms, add an uppercase **OR** between the terms. For example, if you wanted information about Princeton or Harvard University, you could search by **university Princeton OR Harvard**. Just make sure you use an uppercase OR.

Searching all the pages of an entire website
If you wanted to bring up a listing of every page for a certain site, you can use the **site:** search string. An example would be **site:www.onlinecomputertips.com**, which would list every page on the onlinecomputertips.com site that was indexed by the search engine. Keep in mind that this may give you more than you need depending on how many pages are indexed.

Domain search
You can also use the **site:** query to search for a specific item within only one specific website by entering the search terms you're looking for, followed by the word "site" and a colon followed by the domain name. For example, here is how you'd find information about Mustangs on the Ford website. Type in **mustang site:www.ford.com.**

When you hear the word domain, that is referring to the main part of the website address. There can be additional text after the domain name such as **microsoft.com**/products where microsoft.com is the domain and products is a subcategory of that domain.

Of course there are many more tricks of the trade you can use to narrow down your searches, but these should be enough to get you the results you are looking for, so give them a try and see how they work for you.

Deciphering Search Results

Searching the Internet is one thing but trying to figure out what the results of your searches mean is a whole other ordeal. For the most part, search engines do a fairly good job of getting you the most accurate results based on your search terms, but they can still be a little confusing. Plus, with the abundance of advertisements being placed everywhere online, you will need to know the difference between a useful result and something that is just trying to get your money.

The results you get will vary depending on what search engine you are using. You may or may not also be presented with other results from your search related to things like shopping or images. For example, figure 4.5 shows a Google search result for the phrase **tan area rug** with its 57,100,000 results.

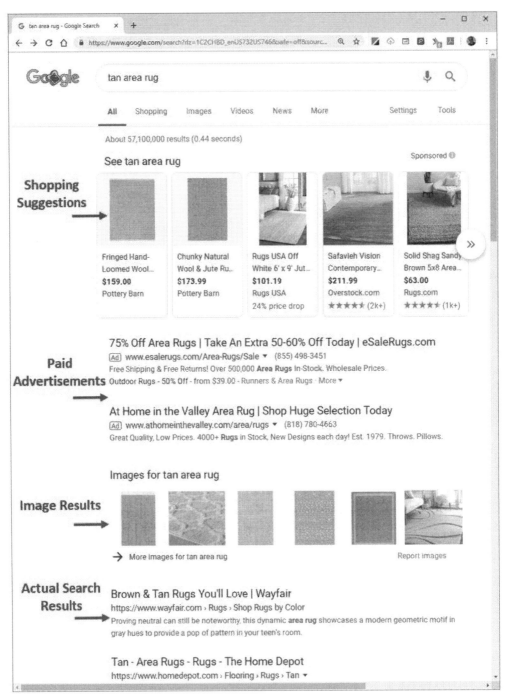

Figure 4.5

The first part of the results shows shopping options that you can click on to find places where you can buy rugs. The next section consists of paid advertisements that other companies pay Google to display when people search for things that apply to them. You can tell these are advertisements because they have the word

Ad next to the address. These may or may not be what you are looking for, and just because they come up at the top of the search results doesn't mean they are the best choice to click on.

Next, you will get image results that match your search in case you were wanting to see images related to tan area rugs. (This would be more useful if you were doing a search for something a little more exciting like beach vacation spots.) Finally, you get the actual search results where you can start looking for the websites that will give you the information you are looking for.

At the bottom of the page (figure 4.6) you might see you may also see more ads at the bottom. At the *very* bottom you will get some suggestions for related searches that you might want to use to improve your search results. You can click on any of them to do a search for that phrase.

If you take a look at the bottom of figure 4.6 you will see that there are many pages of search results that you can go through to find what you are looking for (numbered 1 through 10 and so on). Many people tend to only look at the first page or two because as you get into some of the later pages the results tend to not be as relevant, but that doesn't mean they aren't worth checking out.

Figure 4.6

Now I will perform the same search using the Yahoo search engine to see what their results look like. To do so, I will need to go to the Yahoo website, which is yahoo.com, or I can just do a search from Google for Yahoo. Figure 4.7 shows the results of the search but notice how the layout differs from what Google gave me. You still get similar items such as paid advertisements and shopping suggestions, but they are laid out differently.

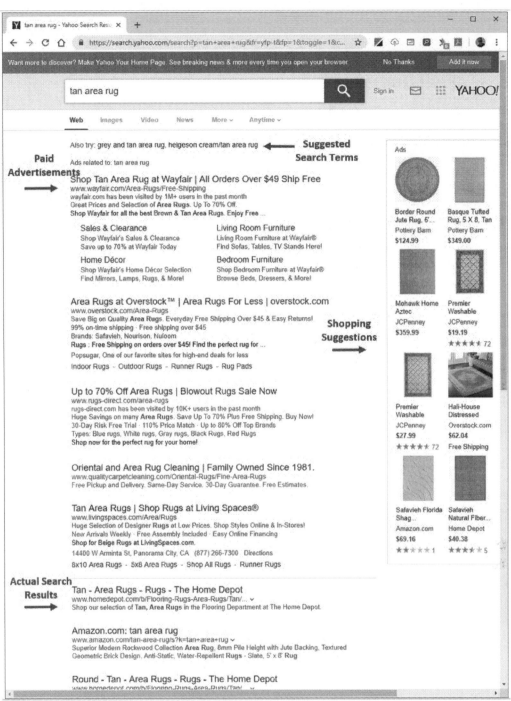

Figure 4.7

If you look at the top of figure 4.7 you will see that Yahoo is asking if I want it to be my default search engine (I use Google for that). If I were to say yes, then it would change the home page of my web browser to the Yahoo website, so be careful when presented with these types of questions.

Figure 4.8 shows the bottom of the page for the Yahoo search results. Once again, there are more paid advertisements, suggested search terms, and additional page numbers. Notice at the bottom right how there are only 9,300,000 results compared to the 57,100,000 results from Google.

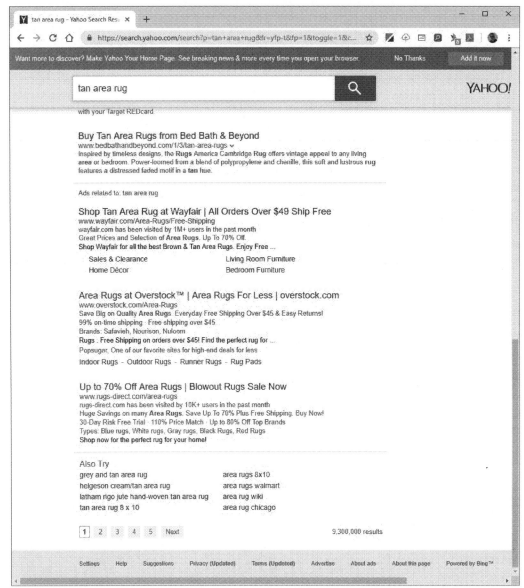

Figure 4.8

As you can see, you will get varying results for your searches based on what search engine you use, so you might want to try out a few to see which one you like the best. It doesn't matter what web browser you are using, and you will get the same results if you are doing your searches on Google using Edge, Firefox, Safari, etc.

Now I would like to talk about the other categories that you can click on for your search term that most search engines offer. Figure 4.9 shows a search for **sailboat** in Google but take a look at the categories below the search box. You can click on any one of them to search within that category.

Figure 4.9

For example, if I click on **Images**, I get the results show below. Notice how there are other ways to fine-tune the image search above the results such as only displaying clipart or wooden sailboats.

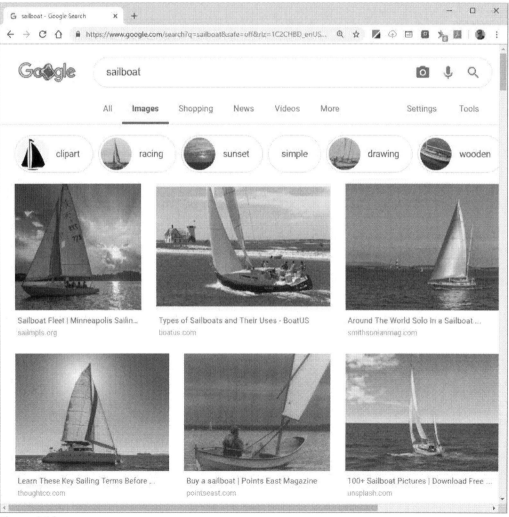

Figure 4.10

Next, I will click on **Shopping**, and here is what I get.

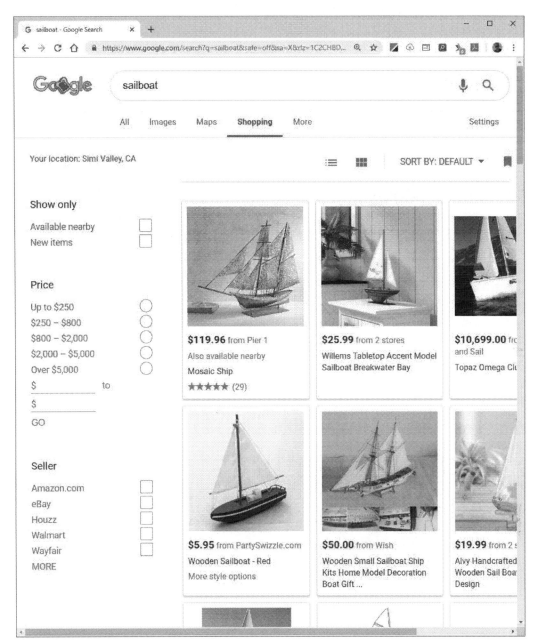

Figure 4.11

Now I will click on **Videos** to see what types of videos there are out there related to sailboats.

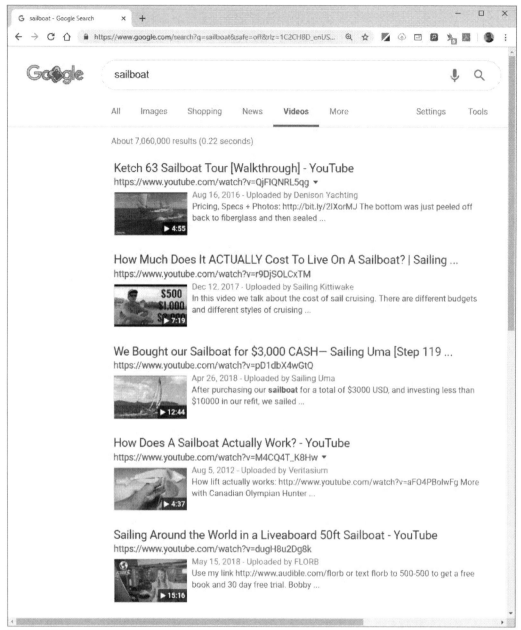

Figure 4.12

Then there are other categories you can choose from, and they can vary depending on what search engine you are using.

So, as you can see, it's fairly easy to get different types of information from your search, so you can find pretty much anything you are looking for.

Saving Pictures and Text from Websites

When searching for things on the Internet, you might feel the need to want to save a particular image or paragraph of text to use later in an email or document etc. This is a very easy process to do, but just like with everything else, the process can vary depending on what web browser you are using and if you are on a Windows PC, Mac, or mobile device.

If you are doing a specific image search, then I suggest that you use the images feature of whatever search engine you are using for the best results. Once you find the image, you want to make sure that you are saving the best quality version and not just a smaller thumbnail version. For example, if you look at figure 4.13, you will see a bunch of Australian Shepherd dog images, and let's say you want to save the first one. If you did save it, then it would be a lower quality\smaller image than you would get if you clicked on it to have it show full size (like in figure 4.14).

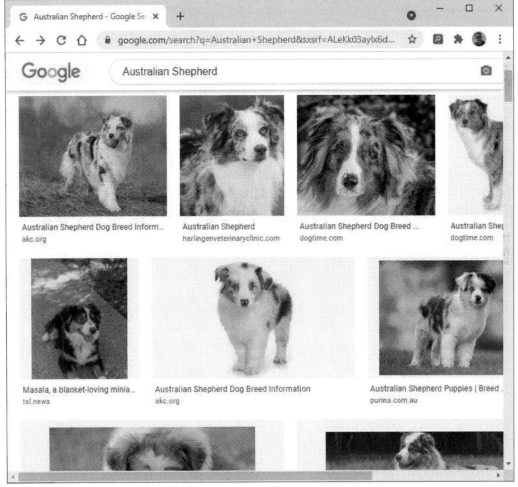

Figure 4.13

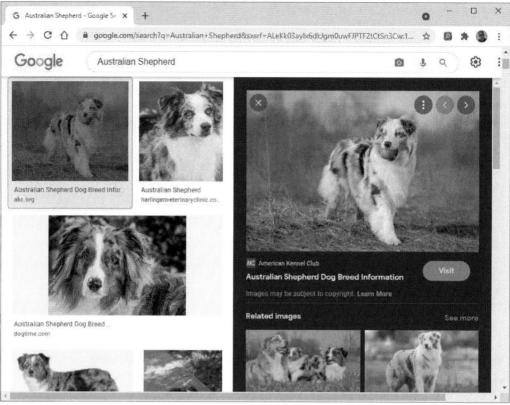

Figure 4.14

If you want to see the image full size, you can right click on it and choose *Open image in new tab*, and it will show the image by itself at its real size. Like I mentioned earlier, your results will vary based on what web browser you are using and what search engine. For my examples, I am using Google's search engine with the Google Chrome browser.

Figure 4.15

Now that I have the image full size, it's time to save it to the hard drive on my computer so I can use it later. To do so, right click anywhere on the picture and choose *Save image as* (or save picture as) and select a location on your computer that you will remember and be able to find later. You can also stick with the default file name, or type in anything you wish. Many people just save images to their desktop or pictures folder.

Figure 4.16

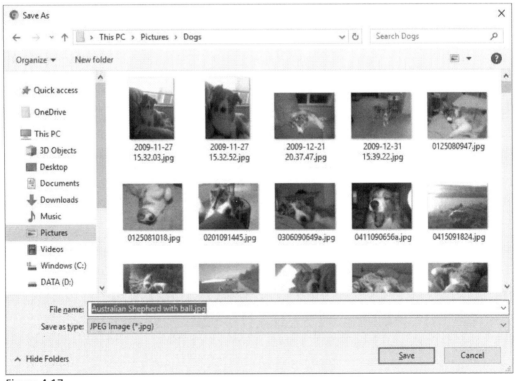

Figure 4.17

 If you ever find an image that doesn't have any save options when you right click on it, it is most likely because they have disabled the saving feature for that web page. Not everyone wants to share their pictures, and it's not always legal to use other people's images for your own work.

When it comes to saving text from a website, it is a much simpler process, and if you can copy and paste text from a document or email, then you shouldn't have any problem with this procedure.

Let's say I am on a particular website and found some useful information that I want to include in a document I am creating on mountain bike trails. I have found the website I want to get the information from and have located the text that I want to save. So, all I need to do is use my mouse to highlight the text (as shown in figure 4.18), then right click anywhere on the highlighted text and choose Copy. (I can also use the *Ctrl-C* keyboard shortcut for Windows users, or *Command-C* for Mac users.)

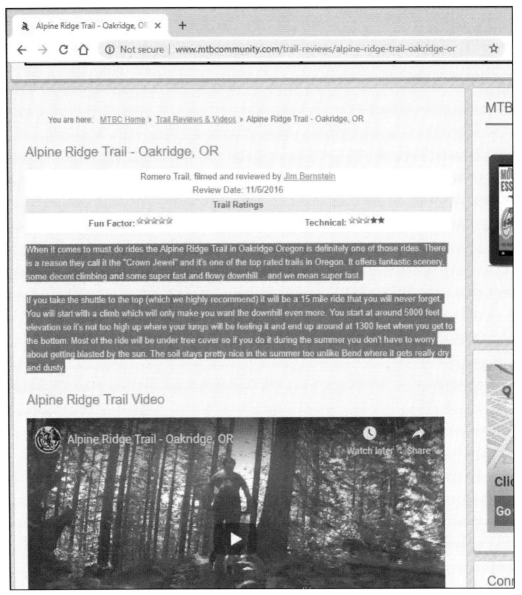

Figure 4.18

Now I want to save the text I copied into a Microsoft Word document, so I go over to my Word document and paste it in. I can either right click where I want the text to go and choose Paste, or I can use the *Ctrl-V* shortcut for Windows or *Command-V* shortcut for Mac.

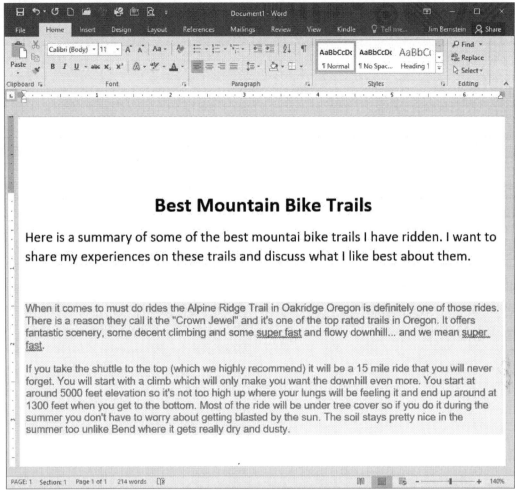

Figure 4.19

One issue you might run into is that when you paste the text wherever you may want to place it, it will most likely keep the text formatting of the web page and not match up with the rest of your document (as you can see in figure 4.19). If this happens, then you will have to highlight the text that you just pasted in and change the font and formatting to match your other text. Or you can use the *paste as plain text* option from the program you are pasting the text into. How you do that will depend on the program, but many times you will have that option when using the *right click>Paste* option.

Finding Directions and Using Online Maps

One of the best things about the Internet is the ability to find the things you need quickly, and finding directions is at the top of the list (at least for me!). Back in the old days, if you wanted to get somewhere, you would either need to call for directions and write them down on a piece of paper, or break out the old map and try and figure it out. Now it's as simple as putting in the destination address of where you want to go and hitting the road.

If you have used the GPS on your phone for directions, then you should already be familiar with this process. One difference between your phone and your computer is that your phone knows where you are, but your computer most likely doesn't. Some services (like Google, for example) will let you set a home location in your profile so that when you are logged into your Google account in your browser, it will use it to find things around you that you are searching for. For example, if you do a search for steak houses, it will find the ones in your area and display them in your search results and also on a map. Then you can click on the one you want to get more information about it and also get directions right to it.

Once again, I will be using the Google search engine and the Chrome web browser to demonstrate how to find directions to a specific location. In this example I want to find out how to get to the Space Needle in Seattle. To begin, I will open up Chrome, click on the apps section at the top right (9 dots), and then on *Maps* (figure 4.20). You can also type in *maps* in your search box from whatever search engine you like to use, and you can use whatever map service you like such as Bing Maps or Yahoo Maps etc.

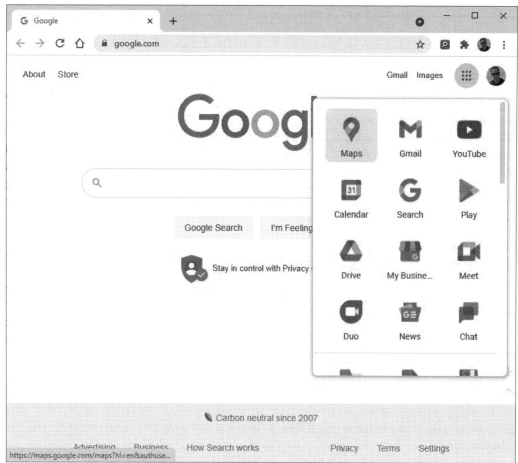

Figure 4.20

Once you open Google Maps, it will take you to your current location (if it knows where you are). You will also have the opportunity to set a home and work address if you like. The home address is used when getting directions to tell you how long it will take from home because it assumes that is where you will be starting from. The work address is used to tell you how long it will take to get to work depending on traffic conditions. You can also click on the buttons for restaurants and hotels etc. as seen in figure 4.21 to find those types of places near where you are searching.

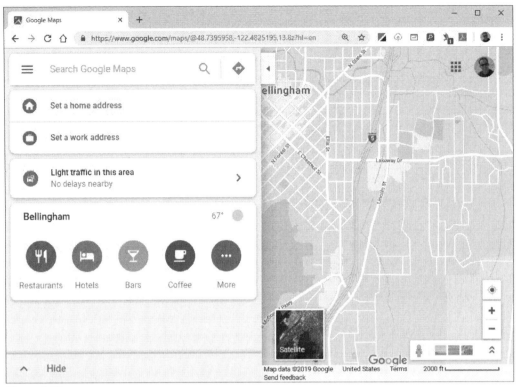

Figure 4.21

Now I will begin my quest to the Space Needle by typing in *Space Needle* in the search box. This will work because Google knows about the Space Needle, and if there were more than one, it would give me a list to choose from. It won't give you results for things like *Frank's house* because it doesn't know who you are talking about. In that case, you would need to type in Frank's address.

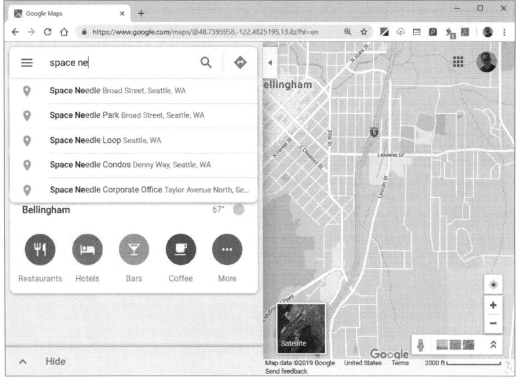

Figure 4.22

As I type in *Space Needle* it starts giving me suggestions, and I can simply click on the one I want if it appears in the list rather than type in the rest of the name. I will click on the first result since I know that is the one I am looking for.

Figure 4.23 shows what I got after choosing my destination. It shows the location on the map marked by a red marker, and also shows me points of interest around the Space Needle. You can scroll around the map and zoom in and out as needed with your mouse wheel (or pinch to zoom on your mobile device).

Take a look at all the options you get at the bottom left of the window. You can do things like get directions, save, see what's nearby, have the directions sent to your phone, and also share the location with other people. I really like the *Send to your phone* option because if you are logged in with your Google account, you can have the location sent right to your phone and then start your navigation immediately without having to search for the location on your phone.

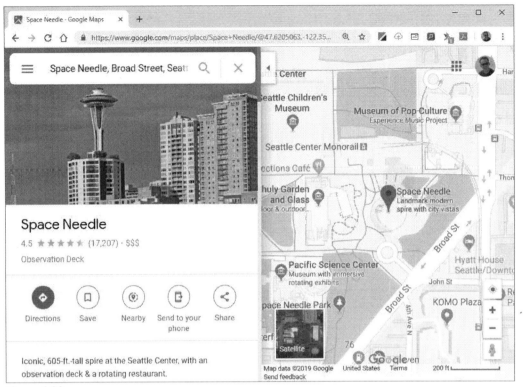

Figure 4.23

When I click on *Directions,* I am prompted to enter the starting point, or in other words where I will be leaving from. I am going to enter *Whidbey Island* so you can see what happens if there are multiple ways to get to a specific location. Figure 4.24 shows me that there are two ways to get there. One involves taking the 5 freeway, while the other one involves taking the 405 freeway. It will highlight the fastest route, but still tell you the time and distance for each route to get there. The time it takes to get there will be based on the current traffic at the time of your search, so if you are planning on going later on in the day, it probably won't be accurate.

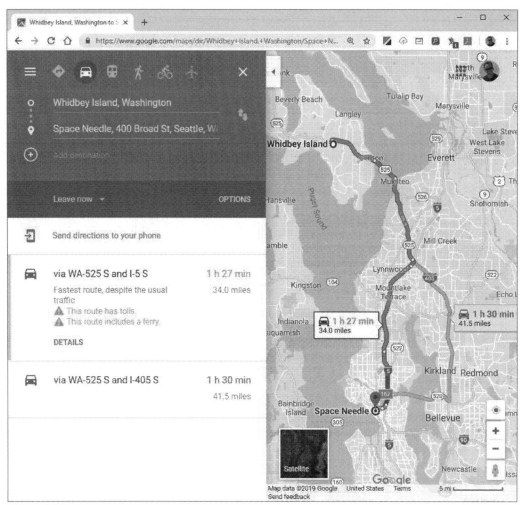

Figure 4.24

By default, Maps will assume you are driving, but if you look at the top of figure 4.24, you will see there are other options such as bus routes, riding a bike, or even walking. Figure 4.25 shows what happens if I click on the bus option.

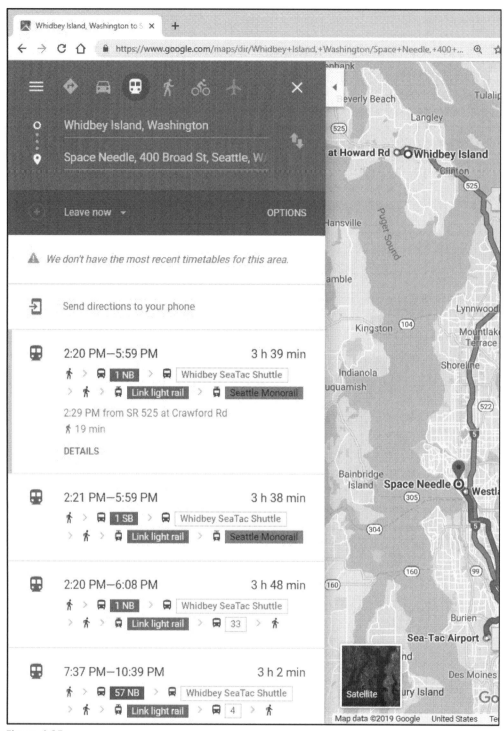

Figure 4.25

As you can see, the results change dramatically, and you now have bus schedules and the time it will take for each bus to make the trip.

Now I would like to discuss the different views you can use within Maps. I will first go to the town of Bellingham, WA and show you what Maps initially shows me (figure 4.26). It will tell you information such as the current weather, provide some photos, and also some quick facts about the area.

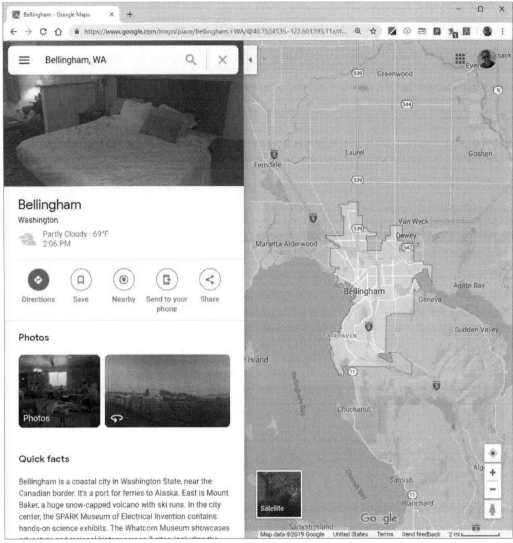

Figure 4.26

If I click on the three horizontal lines at the top of the page, it will give me many more options as to what I can do within the map.

Figure 4.27

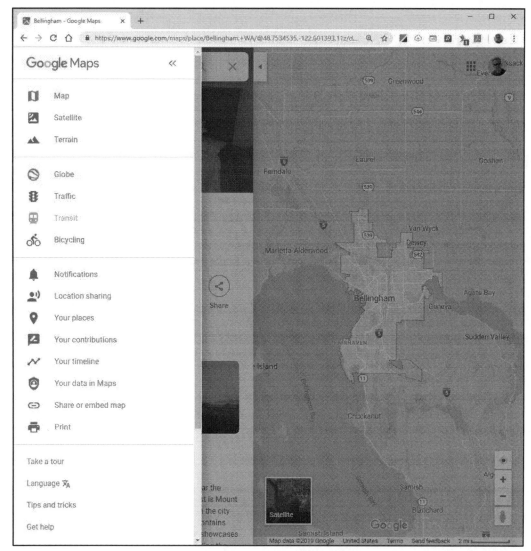

Figure 4.28

I won't go through each of these items since you may not even use Google maps but rather a different map searching service. Plus, you can go through them on your own because that is a great way to learn what each item does.

I do want to show you the traffic feature since this comes in very handy when planning your trips. If you turn on the traffic layer, it will show you the current traffic on the part of the map where you are currently looking. Once again, this is the current traffic, and it most likely won't be the same later, so always have a look at the map right before you leave. As you can see in figure 4.29, it shows different colors for the levels of traffic even though you can't see the colors in this book if you are reading the paperback! Green is for free-flowing traffic, then orange is for mild traffic. Then you get to red for heavy traffic and dark red for very heavy traffic. The more you zoom into the map, the more detailed the traffic report will be.

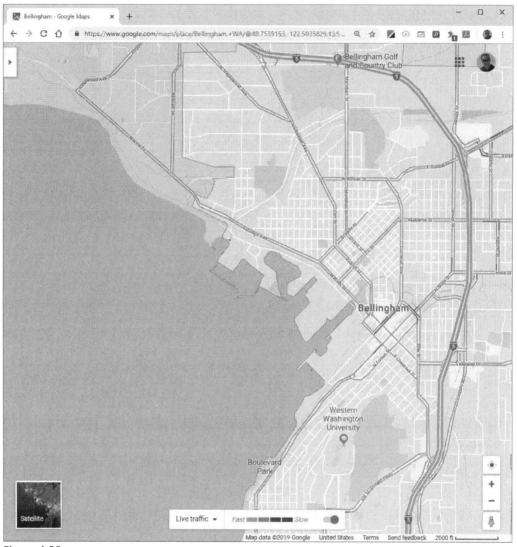

Figure 4.29

Next, I want to show you the satellite mode that Maps offers. This comes in handy if you want to see a photographic view of the area on the map so you can see landmarks that might not show up on the default map view. Plus, you can see the actual buildings and roads using satellite view. To access the satellite view simply click on the satellite icon at the bottom left of the screen as seen in figure 4.29.

Figure 4.30

The more you zoom in, the more detailed the map becomes, and to show you this I went back to the Space Needle and zoomed in a bit (as you can see in figure 4.31).

Figure 4.31

One really cool feature of Maps is the ability to look at what they call *Street View*. Here you can see the actual view from the street outside of where you are looking at. Take a look at figure 4.31 in the lower right hand corner. You can take the little orange person figure at the bottom right of the screen and drag it onto a place on the street to get a street view of that location. The results are shown in figure 4.32. From there you can pan around and zoom and even go up and down the street.

Figure 4.32

You won't have the ability to do this on all streets if they have not been mapped by Google yet. You might have seen those Google maps cars driving around with the strange looking gear on the roof. These are used to map out streets to be using with their mapping service.

Figure 4.33

Sharing Websites with Other People

There will be many times when you are browsing the Internet and come across a website that you want to share with other people, and fortunately this is a very easy thing to do and there are a few ways to do so.

The easiest way to share a website is to copy the site's address and then paste it into something like an email or instant message chat box. If you know how to copy and paste text from something like a document, then this will be a piece of cake for you. Or if you read the section in this chapter about saving text from a website, then the same steps apply here, but the only difference will be what you are copying and pasting.

To copy a website address, what you need to do is click inside the address bar of your browser while on the page you want to share to have it highlight the address. Then you can right click anywhere on the highlighted area and choose *Copy* from the menu (as seen in figure 4.34). You can also use the shortcut keys that I have previously mentioned (Ctrl-C and Ctrl-V).

Figure 4.34

Then you will need to open up your email or the messaging program that you want to use to share the website address, paste it in there, and send it to the person or people you want to share it with. They can then click on the link from that email or message and be taken to that exact same web page.

Streaming Movies and Music
One of the most commonly performed activities that people do on the Internet is stream movies and music. With today's super-fast Internet speeds, it's easy to stream movies and TV shows in high quality HD format, as well as listen to all of your favorite music without having to break out the old stereo system.

There are many upon many ways to get your favorite movies, TV shows, and music on your various devices, and trying to figure out what's best for you and your budget can get a little overwhelming. I would recommend using your newfound searching skills to see what's out there and find some real personal reviews to give you a better idea of what's best for you.

You might have heard of services such as Netflix and Hulu for movies and TV and Pandora and Spotify for music, but there are many more services out there that offer similar content. You will need to decide if it's movies you are looking for or just certain TV shows and find out what providers offer what you need. It's unlikely that you will find one service that offers everything you are looking for, so you will either need to make some sacrifices or get more than one service subscription.

Another thing to consider is if the service you choose is supported on all of your devices and that there is either no limit or a reasonable limit on how many of your devices you can access your account from. For example, if you sign up for a movie streaming service and it will only allow you to register five of your devices (computers, tablets, smartphones, etc.) and you have six devices, then you will not be able to watch movies on one of them. Computers and mobile devices are pretty straightforward to get working with streaming services because you generally either just go to their website or launch their app to get yourself going.

Streaming movies and music requires data to travel back and forth between your device and where the movie or music is coming from. This back and forth action requires what is called bandwidth. Bandwidth is the amount of information that can be sent from one point to another in a certain period of time. The higher the quality of the movie you are viewing, the higher the bandwidth that will be required to get it to your device and have it be nice and clear.

Most home Internet connections are more than fast enough to handle HD (high definition) movies and quality music streaming. However, if you are unlucky enough to have a slow internet connection (such as satellite Internet if you are in a rural location), then you might suffer the consequences with lower quality images or having your movie pause to catch up with itself (this is called buffering).

To use streaming services, you will need to have an account that you can log into with a username and password. Then you can go to the website for that streaming service and log in and then watch your movies or listen to your music. Many times, you can log in with someone else's account if they allow it to watch movies or listen to music.

YouTube and Other Video Sites
YouTube can technically be called a streaming site, but it's not the same as the others that I mentioned earlier because the videos that are available for viewing on YouTube are made by other Internet users such as yourself, and then uploaded to the site for others to watch. These videos can be as pointless as someone

filming their cat sleeping, to something super informative such as a step by step tutorial on how to build a computer. Believe it or not, there are 300 hours of new videos uploaded to YouTube every minute!

When you go to the YouTube website (www.youtube.com) you will see things like recommended and suggested videos that YouTube thinks you may like. These are based on previous videos you have watched if you have been there before. If not, then they will just suggest some trending videos for you to watch.

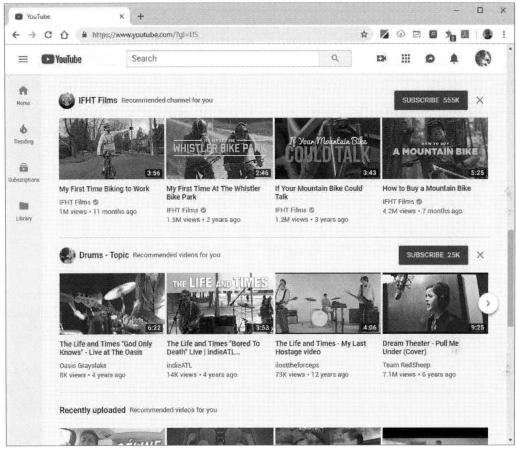

Figure 4.35

YouTube works the same way as a web browser where you type in a search for what you want to find. Figure 4.36 shows the results when I type in *dog tricks* for my search.

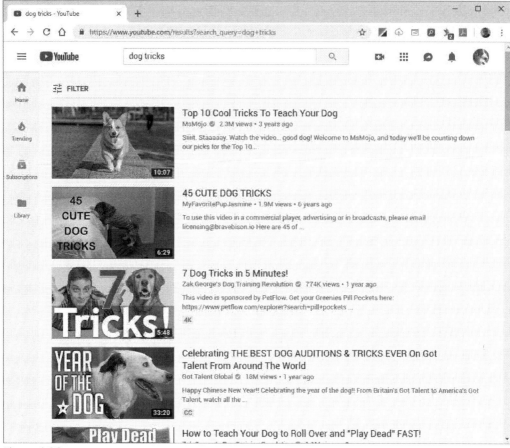

Figure 4.36

If you click on *Filter* at the top left, you will be able to tell YouTube how you want the results displayed and you can have it sort on things such as when it was uploaded, how long it is, or the quality of the video itself, etc.

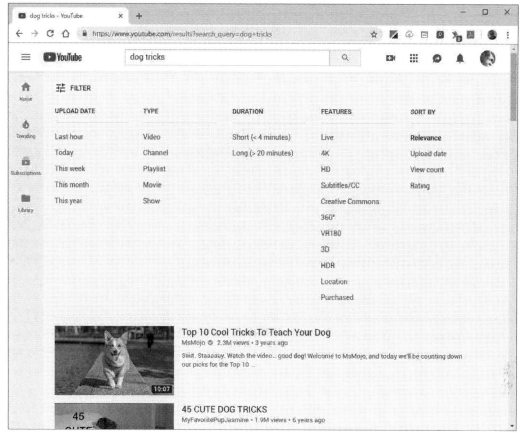

Figure 4.37

When you click on a video to play it, you will be given suggestions for recommended videos based on what you are watching on the right that you can also watch. Just be careful not to get stuck watching videos all day, because it's really easy to do!

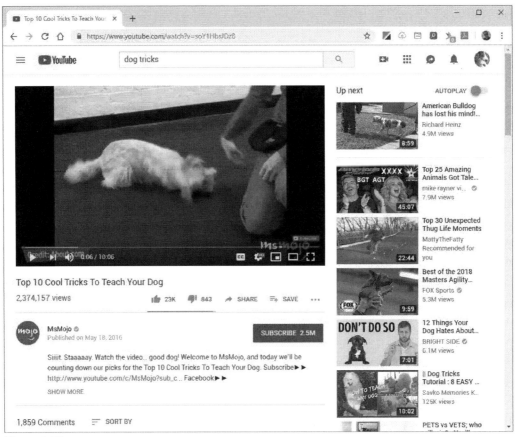

Figure 4.38

When you watch a video, you will notice several icons at the bottom of the video screen. Figure 4.39 shows you what each one does, and it should be pretty self-explanatory. If you want to fast forward a video, you can simply put your mouse cursor on the video time location bar and move it forward or backward.

Figure 4.39

Figure 4.40 shows what each of the sections below the video is used for.

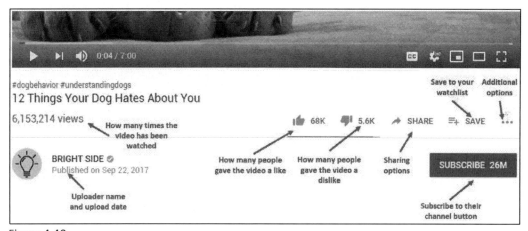

Figure 4.40

For the most part, these should be easy to understand, but I will go over a few that might not be so straightforward. The *Sharing* option will let you do things such as share the video on social media sites like Facebook and Twitter and also allow you to share it via email and with other methods. The *Subscribe* button will add your YouTube account to that particular user's subscription list, and when they release new videos, you will be notified via email. The *Save* option lets you save the video to a watch list that you can go back to later and view it when you want. The three dots will give you other options such as reporting an inappropriate video or viewing a transcript of the audio in the video (as shown in figure 4.45).

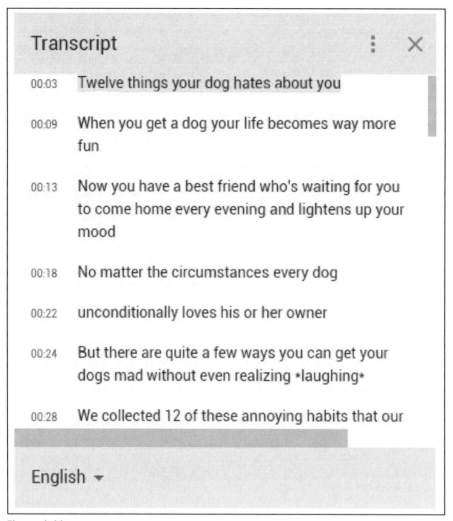

Figure 4.41

Online Shopping

One of the best parts of the Internet is the ability to shop for pretty much anything you will ever need all from the comfort of your chair at home (or, for many, at the office!). There are so many ways to buy so many different types of things from around the world, and once you find them, you can have them shipped right to your door, sometimes the next day!

Thanks to online shopping, you no longer need to drive from store to store to find what you are looking for. Even if you plan on getting your item from a local store, you can still shop for it on their website and even buy it online and then pick it up at the physical store the same day. Or, if you want to send someone a gift, then you can ship the item directly to their house instead of yours.

Many physical stores will even price match with deals you find online, so if you would rather get your item locally but pay the online price, then that is one way to go. (For the most part, this is usually available with larger retailers, and the online price needs to be from a reputable site.)

Popular Shopping Sites
There are many upon many online stores that offer anything you can imagine, but that doesn't mean that they are all the same and that you should whip out your credit card for the first one you come across. The more popular shopping sites are popular for a reason. They provide a wide selection at competitive prices while offering reliable shipping, secure transactions, and easy returns if necessary.

This doesn't mean that you should only stick to the more common shopping sites, but if you are new to online shopping, you might want to give them a try first since they tend to be run more professionally and easier to use. Plus, you can most likely get help from friends who have used the site as well since they are more commonly used.

Amazon
The most popular shopping site of all at the moment is amazon.com, and they have been the most popular for many years now. You can find just about anything you need on Amazon and have it shipped to you in record time if you like. Since it's so popular, I will spend some time going over the site so if you decide to make an account for yourself or already have one, you will have a better idea of how to get around and make the most of your shopping experience.

Figure 4.42 shows the main Amazon website, and yours will not look exactly the same since the site changes constantly with new ads displayed and also products shown that are based on what Amazon thinks you may be interested in. One thing that *will* stay constant is the items on the top of that page that you use to navigate the site itself.

The first thing I want to point out at the upper left hand corner of the page is how in my example it says Amazon Prime. Prime is an additional service or subscription that you can sign up for that gives you benefits such as no minimum order for free shipping, free two day and even same day delivery, music streaming, free movies and TV shows, and so on. The cost of Prime is $119 per year or $12.99 per month. College students can get Prime Student for $59 per year (or $6.49 per month).

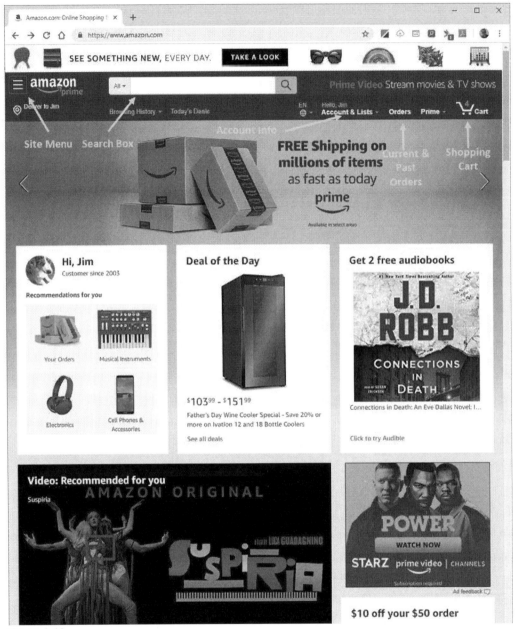

Figure 4.42

The Amazon site menu options can be accessed from the three horizontal bars in the upper left corner. From there, you will have many items to choose from such as searching for videos and music, searching for particular products, and browsing Amazon services. Take some time and go through the choices that sound interesting to you so you can get an idea of what you can do on the site.

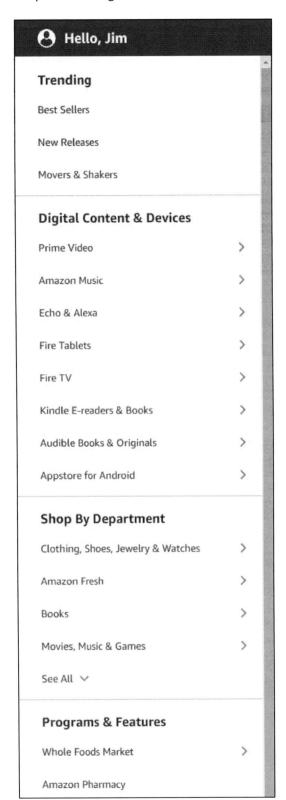

Figure 4.43

The search bar works the same way it does when using a search engine like Google or Bing, but in this case, you can only find things that are available on the Amazon website. If you do a search for something like *weather*, you most likely won't get the results you are looking for! Figure 4.44 shows the results when searching for blenders. As you can see, you get the results in the main section of the page and you will get many pages of results for an item as common as a blender. Fortunately, you can sort by price, customer reviews, and newest arrivals.

Figure 4.44

On the left hand side of the page, you will have other options to help narrow down your search. If you are a Prime member, you can have it only show results that are Prime eligible. Or you can narrow it down by department or brand if the results are too vague. I like how you can also have it show results based on their average customer review, so if you want to see blenders that have a four star rating or higher, for example, you can do that by clicking on the four star review section under *Avg. Customer Review*.

Accounts and Lists is where you can check your account settings and set preferences to enhance your shopping experience. For the most part, you won't do much in here, but if you need to do things like change your shipping address or email address you would do so from here. It's also where you will go to add or edit payment information such as stored credit cards.

Chapter 4 – Using the Internet

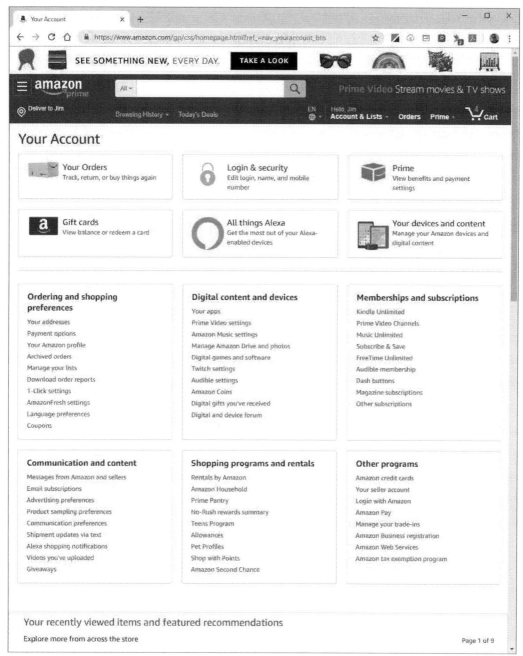

Figure 4.45

Amazon makes it really easy to track your orders and see what you have ordered in the past (which makes reordering items very easy). If you click on *Orders*, it will show you items that you have ordered that are in progress, as well as orders from the past that you have already received. Figure 4.46 shows that I have some items that were just delivered, and also shows that I have placed 100 orders in the past 3 months. I think I have a shopping problem!

125

If you look to the right of any one of the orders you will see that you have many options to choose from. You can track the package if it hasn't been delivered yet, as well as start the return process if you need to send a product back that you don't like or was defective. Once you have purchased an item, you are then allowed to write your own review for that item that others can read.

If you are looking for a particular item that you bought, then you can do a search for it using the *search all orders* box. This comes in handy if you want to reorder something again and want to make sure you get the exact same thing. Then you can click on the *Buy it again* button to reorder the item again.

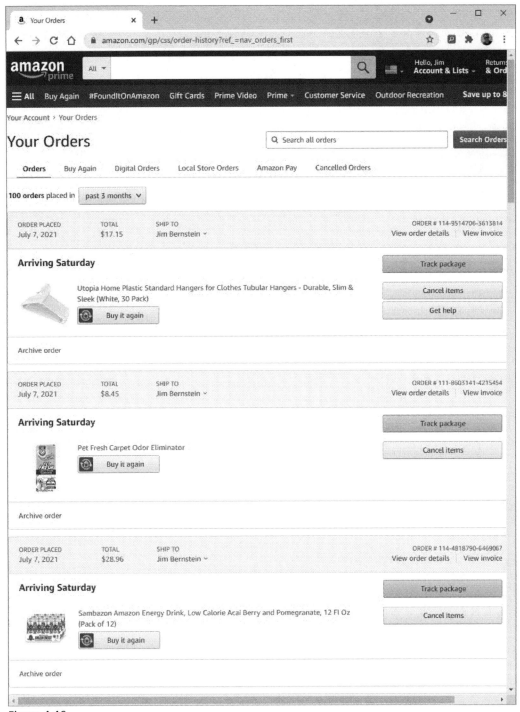

Figure 4.46

If you buy things like music, movies, or software from Amazon, you most likely will have the option to download these types of items directly to your computer so you don't need to wait for them to be delivered. Of course, that means you won't get the physical disk or case, but if you don't need it then this is the way to go. Once you download your order you can go to the *Digital Orders* section to view your purchases and download them again if needed (figure 4.51).

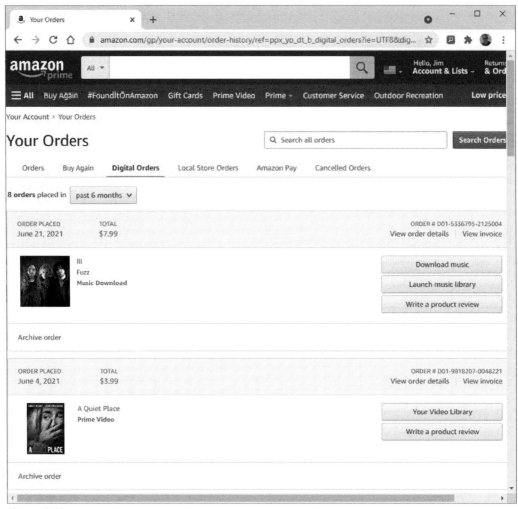

Figure 4.47

Figure 4.48 shows a product page for a blender that I have clicked on. As you can see, you get the description, pictures, and customer reviews for this particular item. It will also tell you the delivery timeframe so you have an idea of when you will get it if you order it. For many items on Amazon you have the option to buy it used, but use your better judgment when doing so, especially on electronics and other things that can stop working. For many items, you can buy a protection plan to extend your warranty in case your item does decide to stop working on you.

There are two options when it comes to buying an item. If you click on *Add to Cart*, it will simply put that item in your virtual shopping cart, and you can check out later and actually make the purchase. If you click on *Buy Now*, it will automatically make the purchase for you using your default shipping address and payment method and bypass the shopping cart.

If you do add an item to your cart, it will show up at the top right in the shopping cart icon (figure 4.49). Then you can click on the cart icon itself to go to your actual shopping cart (figure 4.50).

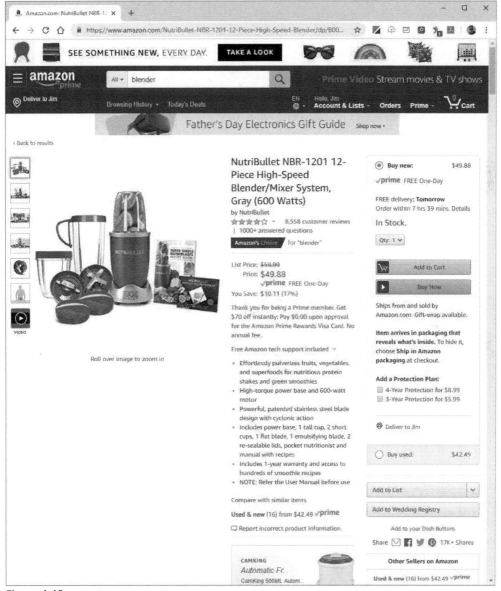

Figure 4.48

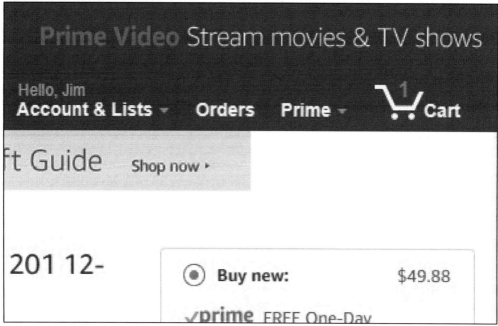

Figure 4.49

Take a look at the options underneath the item in the cart (figure 4.60). As you can see, you can delete the item from your cart, save it for later, or compare it with other items. The save it for later will just move it out of your cart and put it underneath so you can still have it around in case you want to move it back to your cart. As you can see, I have some items in my *saved for later* area.

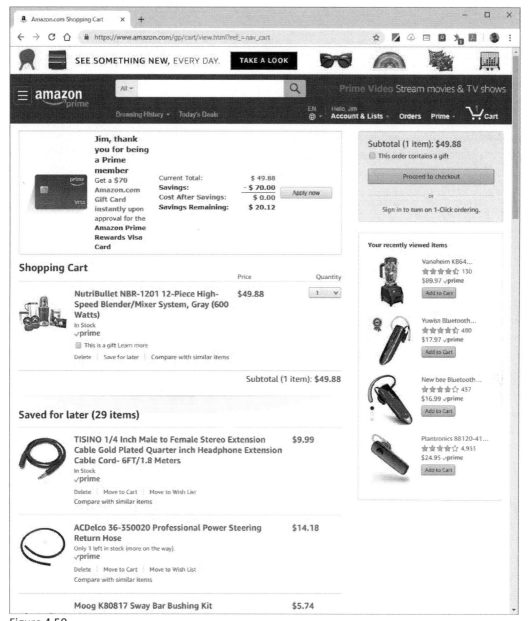

Figure 4.50

When you are ready to buy the items in your cart simply click on the *Proceed to checkout* button and you will see a screen similar to figure 4.51. Then you can confirm your shipping address, payment method, and the items and quantities to be shipped. If you have an Amazon gift card, you can enter the card number under *payment method* to have the gift card amount subtracted from your total.

Section 3 shows your delivery options. Since I have Prime, I can get it delivered to me as early as tomorrow. Sometimes if you want an item faster you will have a choice to pay for expedited shipping if the faster shipping option is not available.

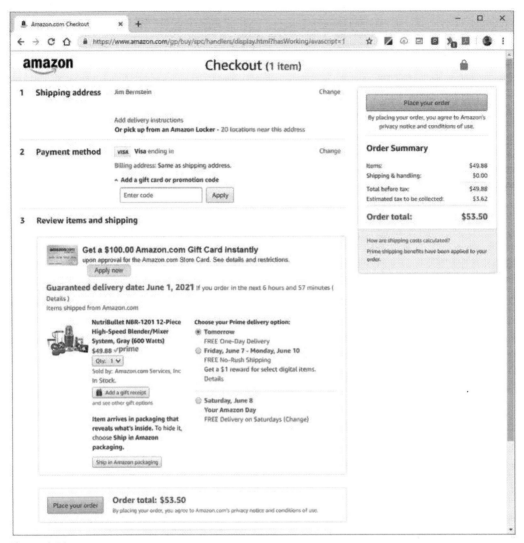

Figure 4.51

If everything looks good, then you can click on the *Place your order* button and then you will be given a confirmation screen that you can review for accuracy. You will also get an email confirmation as well.

Other Sites

There are many upon many other shopping sites online, and some are dedicated to specific products such as electronics or clothing while others offer products from just about any category. Rather than go through more examples from other sites that will look similar to the previous examples, I will just give you a listing of some of the more popular online shopping sites that you can check out for yourself.

- Etsy.com
- Target.com
- Walmart.com
- Overstock.com
- BestBuy.com
- HomeDepot.com

There are also sites such as eBay and Craigslist where you can find new and used items that are being sold by other people. If these products are being sold locally, you can even go pick them up yourself. You need to be very careful when using these sites though because they tend to also be used by scammers looking to steal your money or sell you counterfeit products (especially Craigslist).

I would avoid Craigslist altogether if you can and for eBay make sure you are buying from a reputable seller who has a good rating and reviews. Many retailers will set up online stores on eBay and you can usually find the same products on their actual website.

Search Engine Shopping
Don't forget that you can also shop from your search engine search results like I briefly discussed earlier in this book. So, for example, if I were to search for blenders in Google, I would see the shopping results as seen in figure 4.52. The main difference will be that the results will be from various shopping sites around the globe and not just from one online retailer. If you look at the first result, you can see that under the item title it says *from 50+ stores*, meaning Google found that particular blender for sale from over 50 online retailers.

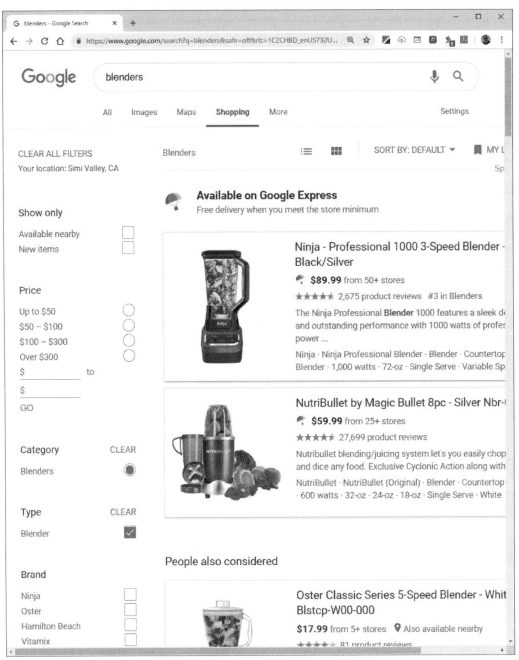

Figure 4.52

Product Reviews

When shopping online or even at your local store, it's nice to be able to find out what experiences other shoppers have had who have purchased the same product that you are interested in buying. Most sites will offer their customers the opportunity to post a review of the product they have bought so that other customers can hear their thoughts on things like the quality of the product, shipping time, and so on.

Product reviews are not what they used to be, and by that I mean you can't trust them as much as you could in the old days. Many companies find ways to alter these overall ratings by doing things such as paying others to post fake reviews or using other mischievous methods. This doesn't mean *all* reviews are fake, but when you see a bunch of five star reviews along with a bunch of one star reviews, it makes you wonder how that product can have that many reviews on both sides of the scale. What I like to do is look at the three and four star reviews to hopefully get the most honest reviews. Of course, many of the five star reviews are valid as well, so it doesn't hurt to read those. I also find that many of the one star reviews are from people who just like to hear themselves complain or had a bad experience that was just a fluke or has nothing to do with the product itself (such as a box that was damaged during shipping).

For my review example, I will go back to Amazon, pick another blender, and show you the reviews for it. Figure 4.53 shows that this blender has 3,355 customer reviews, which is quite a lot of reviews in general. If you look at the stars it shows that the average review rating for this blender is about 4.5 stars.

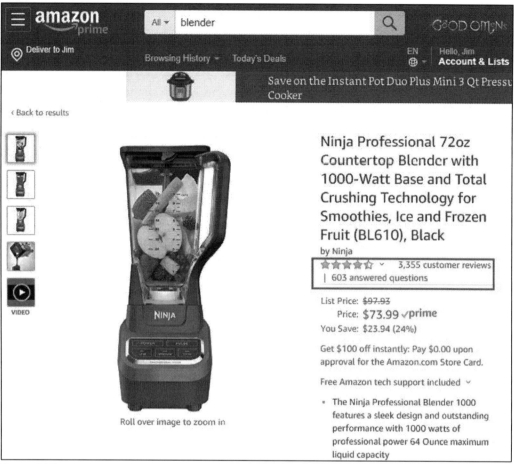

Figure 4.53

Clicking on the down arrow next to the stars will show you the percentage that each star has towards the total rating. If you look at figure 4.54, you will see that 71% of the reviewers gave it a five star rating.

Figure 4.54

Clicking on See all 3,355 reviews will allow you to dig deeper into the reviews and sort or filter the results (figure 4.55). If you want to see all of the one star reviews, for example, then you can click where it says 1 star and see only those results (figure 4.56).

Ninja Professional 72oz Countertop Blender with 1000-Watt Base and... › Customer reviews

Customer reviews

⭐⭐⭐⭐½ 3,355

4.3 out of 5 stars ⌄

5 star		71%
4 star		9%
3 star		5%
2 star		4%
1 star		11%

Ninja Professional 72oz Countertop Blen...

by Ninja

Price: $73.99 ✓prime

Write a review

Top positive review

See all 2,698 positive reviews ›

👤 tallslenderguy

⭐⭐⭐⭐☆ owned 6 weeks

January 5, 2018

I'm a healthcare professional and bought this after researching the competition (i.e., "Vita-Mix). After reading through a gazillion comments and reviews (including CR who rates the Ninja #2) I opted for the lower priced Ninja. I have used mine twice a day for the 6 weeks I have owned it, I use it for making smoothies. I blend for health, I have a morning fruit and berry smoothie and I have an afternoon veggie

Read more

992 people found this helpful

Top critical review

See all 657 critical reviews ›

👤 Leah McFaul

⭐☆☆☆☆ But this is such a horrible blender for what you pay

March 28, 2018

I never write reviews. But this is such a horrible blender for what you pay, I had to write a review. Another reviewer wrote "it takes the smooth out of smoothie" and he couldn't be more right. I'm not sure how this blender got so many good reviews. So many times I tried making my smoothies and açaí bowls and had to stick a spoon in the blender and

Read more

239 people found this helpful

🔍 Search customer reviews   **Search**

SORT BY   **FILTER BY**

| Top rated ⌄ | All reviewers ⌄ | All stars ⌄ | Text, image, ... ⌄ |

Figure 4.55

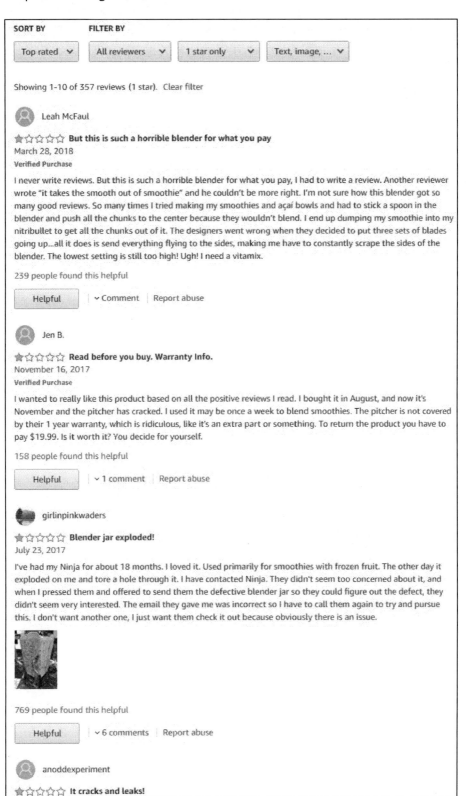

SORT BY   **FILTER BY**

Top rated ∨   All reviewers ∨   1 star only ∨   Text, image, … ∨

Showing 1-10 of 357 reviews (1 star). Clear filter

Leah McFaul

★☆☆☆☆ **But this is such a horrible blender for what you pay**
March 28, 2018
Verified Purchase

I never write reviews. But this is such a horrible blender for what you pay, I had to write a review. Another reviewer wrote "it takes the smooth out of smoothie" and he couldn't be more right. I'm not sure how this blender got so many good reviews. So many times I tried making my smoothies and açaí bowls and had to stick a spoon in the blender and push all the chunks to the center because they wouldn't blend. I end up dumping my smoothie into my nitribullet to get all the chunks out of it. The designers went wrong when they decided to put three sets of blades going up...all it does is send everything flying to the sides, making me have to constantly scrape the sides of the blender. The lowest setting is still too high! Ugh! I need a vitamix.

239 people found this helpful

Helpful   ∨ Comment   Report abuse

Jen B.

★☆☆☆☆ **Read before you buy. Warranty Info.**
November 16, 2017
Verified Purchase

I wanted to really like this product based on all the positive reviews I read. I bought it in August, and now it's November and the pitcher has cracked. I used it may be once a week to blend smoothies. The pitcher is not covered by their 1 year warranty, which is ridiculous, like it's an extra part or something. To return the product you have to pay $19.99. Is it worth it? You decide for yourself.

158 people found this helpful

Helpful   ∨ 1 comment   Report abuse

girlinpinkwaders

★☆☆☆☆ **Blender jar exploded!**
July 23, 2017

I've had my Ninja for about 18 months. I loved it. Used primarily for smoothies with frozen fruit. The other day it exploded on me and tore a hole through it. I have contacted Ninja. They didn't seem too concerned about it, and when I pressed them and offered to send them the defective blender jar so they could figure out the defect, they didn't seem very interested. The email they gave me was incorrect so I have to call them again to try and pursue this. I don't want another one, I just want them check it out because obviously there is an issue.

769 people found this helpful

Helpful   ∨ 6 comments   Report abuse

anoddexperiment

★☆☆☆☆ **It cracks and leaks!**

Figure 4.56

Try to read reviews when shopping online for things, especially if they are costly items, to see what other people think. If you are buying something you have bought before and know you like it, then you can pretty much ignore what others have to say. Just try not to make your decision based solely on what other people think because you might miss out on a great product that would have worked out just fine for you.

Secure Payment Methods
When buying products online, you want to have the safest experience possible, so you don't end up getting ripped off or have your personal information stolen etc. I will be going over online safety in Chapter 11, but for now I just wanted to go over some key concepts when it comes to staying secure when paying for your purchases.

The most important thing to consider when shopping online is to make sure you are shopping on a safe and reputable site to begin with. If the site looks like it was designed by a child and has spelling and grammar errors, then it might be something you want to stay away from. Or, if it's based out of another country that might not be known for its security, then that's another red flag.

One of the most important things to check for when shopping online is that you are on the site you are supposed to be on and that it's a secure website. Anyone can make a website that looks just like amazon.com, but if the address bar doesn't say **amazon.com**, then you know something is wrong. You also want to make sure that there is an **S** at the beginning of the address where it says *https*. If it just says http, then it's not a secure website and you shouldn't be shopping there. Figure 4.57 shows that I am on the amazon.com website and that it's a secure site so I can feel comfortable giving my credit card information to them.

Figure 4.57

Speaking of credit cards, many sites offer you the opportunity to save your shipping and credit card information on the site so you don't need to type in each time you want to buy something. If it's a site you will be using often, then you might want to save your information, but if it's going to be a one-time thing, then I would advise against it. I also wouldn't save debit card information on a site in case your debit card might not have the same type of fraud protection that most credit cards have.

PayPal

There are other ways to pay for items online besides giving them your credit card. Many sites these days will use payment services that allow you to pay them directly from your bank account and bypass using your credit card. One of the most popular online payment services is called PayPal.

PayPal allows you to create an account and link it directly to your bank account to make purchases online. You can keep a balance in your PayPal account if you like, or if you don't have any money in your account it will take it directly from your bank account. You can also link a credit card to your PayPal account if you desire.

When you choose the PayPal payment option on a site it will take you to the PayPal login page where you will sign in with your username and password that you set up your account with, and then approve the transaction. Then it will take you back to the site where you are buying the item from and allow you to finish the transaction. It's as simple as that!

You can also log in to the PayPal site at any time to see things like your balance and recent transactions. If you take a look at figure 4.58 you will see that you get a lot of information right from the Summary page of your account. You can see things like the balance in your account and also the balance in your PayPal Credit account (if you have signed up for one). The PayPal Credit account is like a credit card, so any money that shows up there is money you owe, not money you have to spend!

At the bottom of the page, you will see what bank accounts or credit cards you have linked to your PayPal account. Keep in mind that if you change or cancel one of these accounts, then you will have to update the information in PayPal with your new accounts in order to use them with PayPal.

If you have previously sent someone money, they will show up in the *Send again* section, which is more like a recent transaction section that makes it easy to send that person more money.

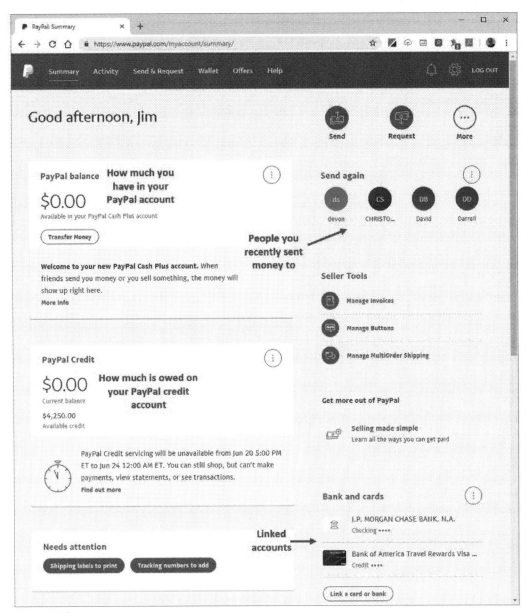

Figure 4.58

Figure 4.59 shows the Activity page where you can see all of the money you have sent and received via PayPal. You can enter in a date range as well if you want to only see results from a certain time period.

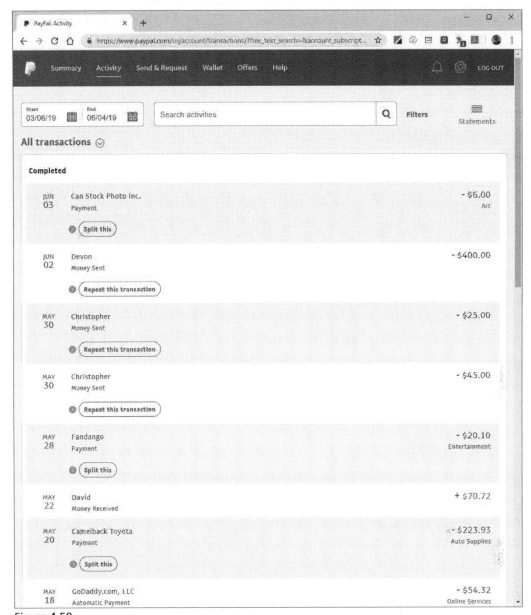

Figure 4.59

One of the great benefits of PayPal is that you can use it to send other people money rather than doing something like sending a check, getting cash out of the ATM, or doing a bank transfer. This also comes in handy for buying things from sites such as Craigslist because you most likely won't be able to use a credit card, and if you use cash then you have no record of the transaction in case there is a problem.

There are two ways to send money to other people via PayPal. You can do the friends and family method, which lets you send money for free, or you can use the pay for item or service method, which will result in a charge for the person on the receiving (selling) end. When you use the pay for item or service method, you get protection from PayPal on your purchase in case you don't get the item after you pay or it's defective. It's not a 100% guarantee that you will be taken care of, but it's a lot better than having no protection at all.

When you click on the *Send & Request* section you can enter that person's email account or phone number that they have associated with their PayPal account. You will need to ask them what address or number to use because you can't just put in anything you like and expect it to work unless it's associated with their PayPal account.

Figure 4.60

Then you will be asked if you are sending to a friend or paying for an item or a service (figure 4.61). If you are sending to someone you trust, then you will use the friend option, so they don't get charged for the transaction. When I say get charged, I mean that PayPal will take a small percentage out of the transaction for themselves. The fee for each transaction is $0.30 plus 2.9% of the amount they are receiving.

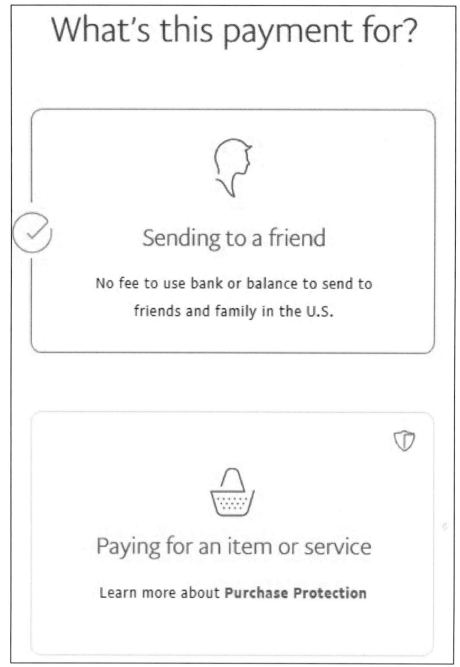

Figure 4.61

PayPal is free to use and has been a safe and effective way to pay for online purchases and for sending people money. It's easy to sign up for, and all you need to do to link your checking account is put in your account number and routing number off one of your checks and you are good to go!

 Venmo is another online payment service similar to PayPal and is actually owned by PayPal. The younger generation seems to like to use Venmo over PayPal because it has more of a social media feel to it. As of right now, you can only send payments via Venmo using their phone application.

Chapter 5 – Online Applications and Services

These days the Internet is used for much more than searching for cute dog pictures and shopping for blenders, which is fine if that's all you care about! But if you want to do more with the Internet, then there are some other tools you can use to make the most productive use of your time. In fact, many businesses run their entire operation online and don't even have a physical location.

Office Applications

I'm sure you have used programs like Microsoft Word or Excel at home and are familiar with how they work and what they are meant to be used for. And FYI, Microsoft is not the only game in town when it comes to these types of programs, but they are the biggest player! Just a few short years ago in order to use these types of programs, you would need to install them on each computer that you wanted to run them on and also have a software license for each one.

These days you can now run your office productivity programs online via your web browser and the Internet. There are several online services that let you run the same types of programs on just about any device that you can connect to the Internet with. But instead of calling them "programs", they usually refer to them as "applications" or "apps" for short.

Rather than go over all of the available apps you can use to do things such as create documents, spreadsheets, and presentations, I will just go over a couple of the most popular ones, which are Microsoft Office 365 and Google Docs since they are at the top of the list when it comes to popularity and functionality.

Office 365 is a subscription-based service from Microsoft that will allow you to use their online applications for a fee. They do have a free version called Microsoft Office for the Web (or Office Online), which doesn't have all the bells and whistles of Office 365 but will probably do the job just fine for many users. As you can see in figure 5.1, Office Online has many built-in apps for things besides documents and spreadsheets such as an email client, calendar, and contact manager. They even offer free online file storage if you want to keep your documents etc. online in "the cloud" rather than on your computer.

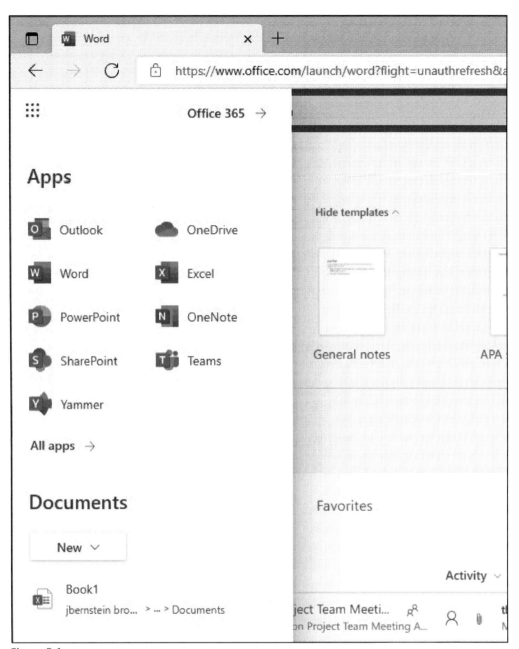

Figure 5.1

For my example, I am going to click on Word Online and open up one of the built-in template documents (as shown in figure 5.2). If you are familiar with the desktop version of Word, you will notice how the toolbar looks very similar to the one you are used to seeing with the regular Word program. You can do things such as change the font, colors, text size, layout, and so on just like in the desktop version. Of course, the desktop version and Office 365 version will have more advanced features, and that's why they are not free!

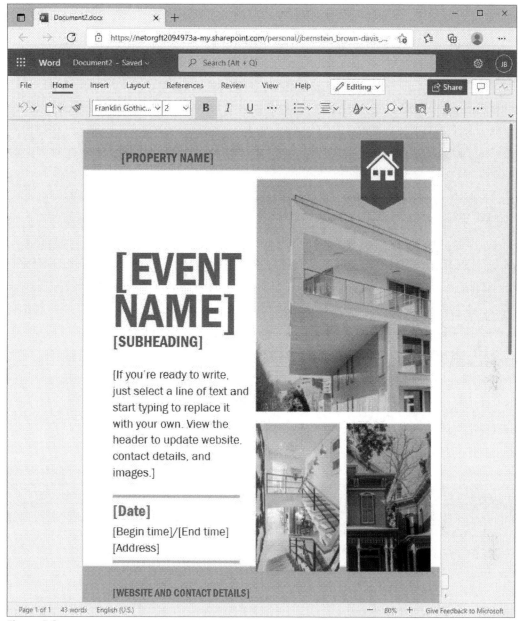

Figure 5.2

By default, Office Online will save your work to your OneDrive online storage account—which you get for free, but if you want to save your work to your computer, then you will need to go to the *Save As* option from the *File* menu, choose *Download a Copy*, and then choose where you want to save the file on your desktop PC.

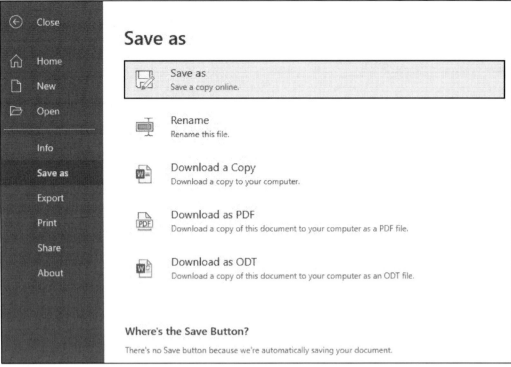

Figure 5.3

One benefit of saving your files to your online storage is that you will have the ability to share them and allow others to collaborate with you without having to email the documents back and forth.

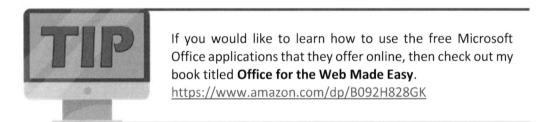

If you would like to learn how to use the free Microsoft Office applications that they offer online, then check out my book titled **Office for the Web Made Easy**.
https://www.amazon.com/dp/B092H828GK

If you are not a fan of the Microsoft Office apps then Google offers a similar service that they call *Google Apps*, and it's free as well unless you want to use the corporate version that they call G Suite, but the free version of their apps should work just fine for you. Figure 5.4 shows the Google Apps menu where you can choose from some of the available applications. There are many more you can use than what is shown here, but in order to get to them, you will have to go to that specific site. For example, if you want to use the Google Calendar then you will need to go to https://calendar.google.com, or just do a search for it and sign in with your Google account.

Once again, I am going to use the Google version of Word (which is called Google Docs) by clicking on it from the available choices. Then I will open one of their built-in template files (figure 5.5).

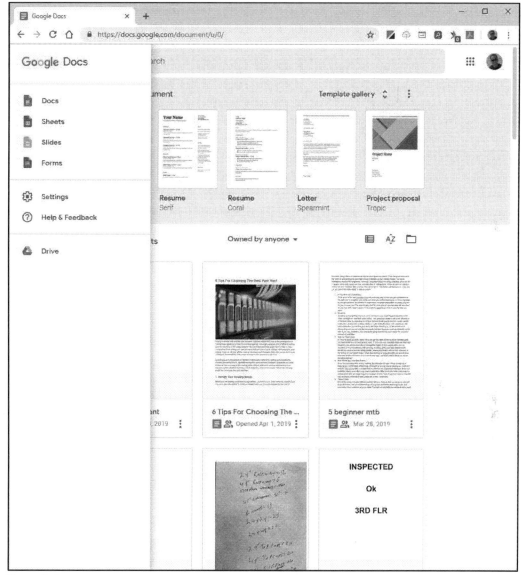

Figure 5.4

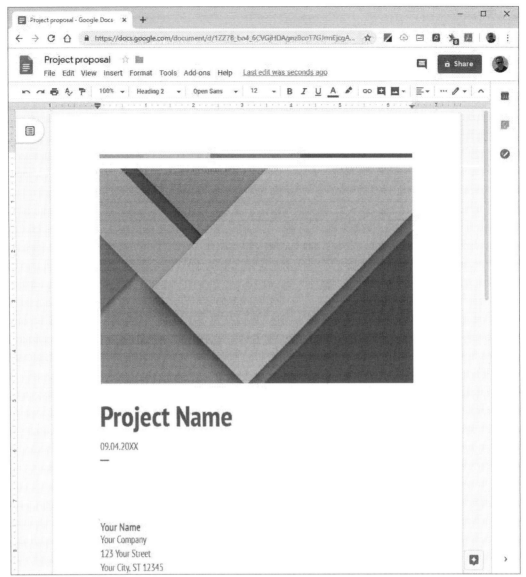

Figure 5.5

As you can see, the interface looks similar to Word Online, and when it comes to saving your files they will go to your Google Drive unless you *specifically* tell Docs to save them to your computer. To do this you will need to go to the *File* menu and then choose *Download as* and pick the format you want to save the file as.

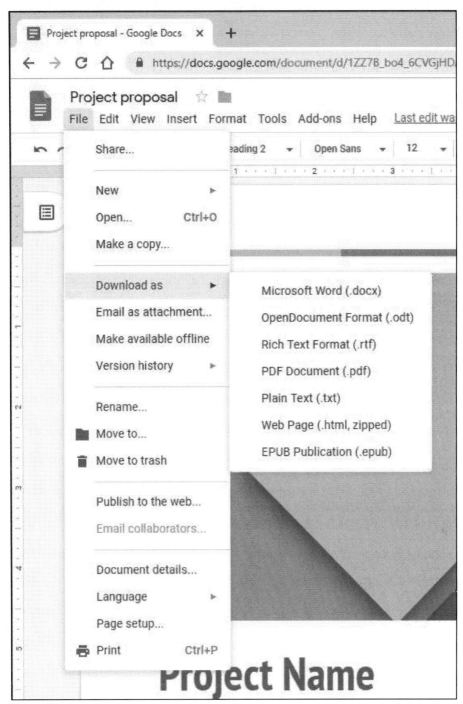

Figure 5.6

 I have recently written a book called **Google Apps Made Easy** that contains everything you need to know to get you up and running with all of the most popular applications that Google offers you to use. You can check it out here: https://www.amazon.com/dp/1798114992

Feel free to play around with these services and applications to see if they are something you want to use for yourself in case you feel like expanding your skillset to include "cloud computing", as it's often referred to.

Online Banking and Bill Paying

One of my favorite things about the Internet is not having to write checks, address envelopes, and buy stamps to pay my bills. And even better, I like how I don't have to get paper bills in the mail that I end up having to shred because I don't need to keep them for any reason. (Plus, all the unnecessary tree killing!) It's also nice to be able to check your credit card balance and purchases any time you want.

Thanks to online banking and bill paying, it's much easier to stay organized and make sure all your bills are paid on time. The only downside is having to risk exposing your information such as account numbers, your social security number, usernames, and passwords online since it's all going over the Internet to a server who knows where. But if you use caution (and common sense), you will be just fine. Plus, most banks and credit cards offer protection against online theft and fraud.

Once you have an account with your bank or utility company, it's very easy to sign up for an online account. Simply go to their website and enter your information to prove it's you. This information might be in the form of an account number, credit card number, name, address, and so on. (Just make sure you are on the official site for that company before giving out any of this information!)

Then once you have your account configured, you simply sign in with the username and password you created, and you are good to go. (Many times your username will be your email address.) Also, be sure to create a complex password to prevent unauthorized people from getting into your account.

It's a good idea to provide your phone number when signing up for an online account because it can be used to verify it's really you when logging in from a new device, or if you need to reset your password in case you forget it.

Figure 5.7 shows a typical credit card site where you can see things such as the balance owed, credit limit, payment information, payment due date, recent transactions, and more. All of this information is at your fingertips any time you need it, and if you want to see something like an older statement, all you need to do is choose an older date.

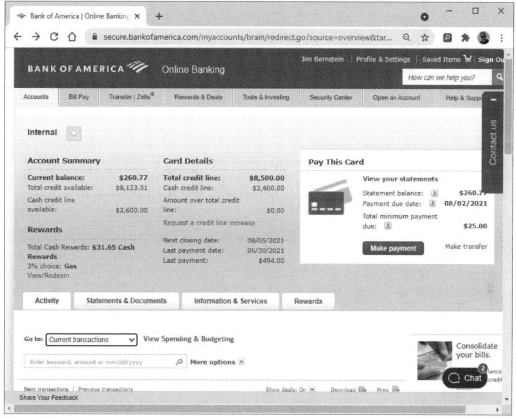

Figure 5.7

To make a payment in this example, you would just click the *Make Payment* button, put in the amount you wish to pay and the date you wish to pay it, and they will take care of the rest. You will need to first set up a payment method such as your checking account beforehand in order for them to have a place to take the money from.

Like I've said before, what you see in my examples will not always look exactly like what you will see when you try this yourself because each website is different, plus the web browser and device you use will make a difference as well. (And yes, I will be saying this again later in the book, so get used to it!).

Online Games

The Internet is not just about doing research and paying bills, but also for having fun and killing (or wasting) time. And what better way to kill some time than with video games? When you think about playing video games, you might think that you need a game console like a PlayStation or Xbox, but there are actually many great games you can play on your computer, smartphone, or tablet.

When playing games on a smartphone or tablet you usually need to install the app for that game and then it will connect you to the Internet so you can play along with other people (if it's in fact that type of game). There are also many games that you can play by yourself without needing to interact with others.

For computer games, you can also have standalone video games that you install like you would any other software, and then play either by yourself or online with other people. If you go the online route, then you will need to have an Internet connection, of course, and for many of these games it's better to have a faster connection to avoid lag (delays) in your games.

The type of online games I want to discuss don't involve purchasing or installing any software to play and are played via your web browser. **One thing I want to stress is if you find a free online game and it wants you to download and install something to play it, then you should say no and get off that website because it's most likely going to install some type of spyware on your computer that will be used to do things like track your web surfing or steal your personal information**.

Since I'm not a "gamer" I can't tell you which gaming sites are the best, but you can do a search for something like *online games* or *free online games* and see what you come up with. As you can see in figure 5.8, I get a mere 15 billion results when I search for online games, so have fun searching through all of the results!

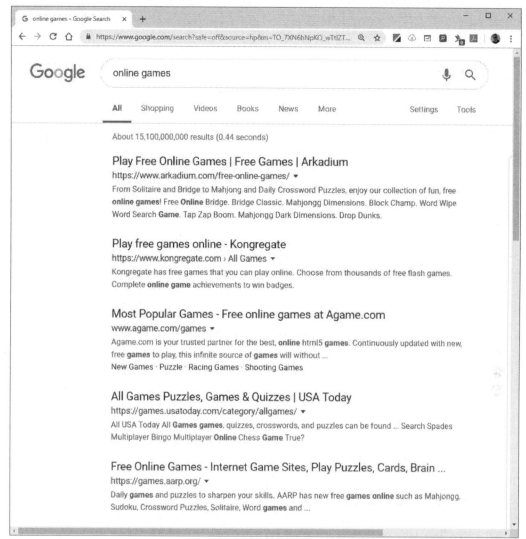

Figure 5.8

Figure 5.9 shows what I get when I click on the first link. As you can see, there are many types of games to choose from, and even a search box where you can search for a particular type of game.

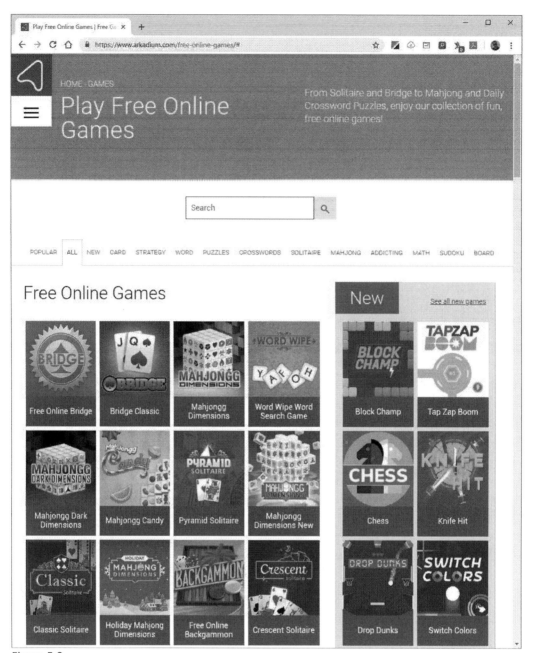

Figure 5.9

Next, I clicked on Classic Solitaire, and then the game loads and I am able to play. Did you notice in figure 5.10 how the screen is filled with advertisements? That is what makes the games free because they are hoping you will click on one of their ads and make some money for them. When you see things like those *Start Now* buttons, they are generally trying to make you think you should click on them to play the game, but it's really only an ad.

Figure 5.10

So just remember to be careful when playing free games online. There is usually a catch because, as we all know, nothing is really free!

 You can also go to the Microsoft Store which I discussed in Chapter 2 where you can download games for free and install them on your computer. There are also versions that cost money so be aware of that before you download any. Also be sure to read reviews before trying any.

Chapter 6 – Social Media

Social media has been a growing part of the online experience for many years now, and if you haven't gotten on the bandwagon, you are missing out (well, that depends on who you talk to!). There are so many social media sites and apps now that it's impossible to cover them all (since some of them disappear as fast as they show up), so I will go over the major players in this chapter.

For the most part, social media is a good way to connect with friends and family that you aren't able to see on a regular basis. It's also a great way to promote something like a business or charity to get more people aware that they exist. (Of course, you also have the people who abuse these sites by promoting illegal and immoral things or by trying to scam others out of money etc.)

Facebook

One of the most popular social media sites in the world is Facebook, which has been around since 2004. From what I've heard from the younger generation, it's not "what the kids are into" these days, but it's still very popular among "older" generations. There is a lot that you can do on Facebook, but I will just go over the most common features to get you up and running so you can decide if you want to be a member or not.

Facebook is a way for you to post stories, pictures, movies, website links, and so on for things that you are interested in or are involved in. Many people use it to do things like post pictures of their pets or vacations or complain about their boss etc., while others use it to make their followers aware of a certain cause that they are passionate about.

When I say followers, what I mean is the people that are following them on the Facebook site. Followers are different from friends. You can follow other people like celebrities, bands or other groups if they allow it but you can't just become "friends" with anyone you want, but have to do what is called a *friend request,* which has to be accepted by the person you have sent the request to. So, if you did a search for Joe Smith and find the Joe Smith you are looking for, you can send him a friend request. Then Joe can either accept or reject that request. If he accepts it, then you will be able to see what Joe is posting on his Facebook page and interact with his posts by doing things such as giving them "likes" and making comments on the posts.

Facebook uses what they call a timeline on your main page that shows you posts from people that you are friends with, and also other people or groups that you follow. For example, if you like the band The Beatles, you can find their Facebook page and then click on Like. You will then be following them and will see their posts in your timeline. For pages like this, you don't need to be accepted in order to see their posts because they are public pages that people (including you) can create in order to get exposure from others. Figure 6.1 shows what I get when searching for The Beatles. You will see results related to posts about The Beatles as well as photos, videos, pages and items for sale related to The Beatles.

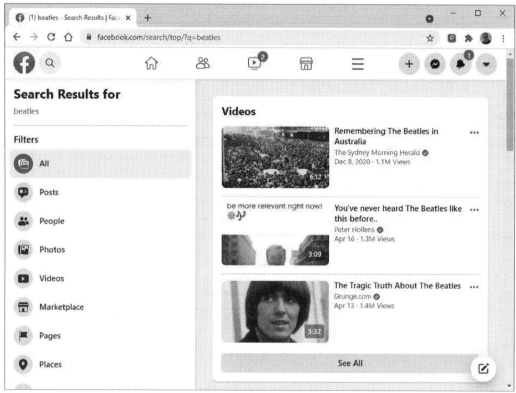

Figure 6.1

If I click on *Pages* on ages the left, I will be shown Facebook pages such as one of their many fan pages, which you can like or follow by clicking on the thumbs up icon to the right of the page name. You can also like the page from that particular page itself once you click on it to view the page.

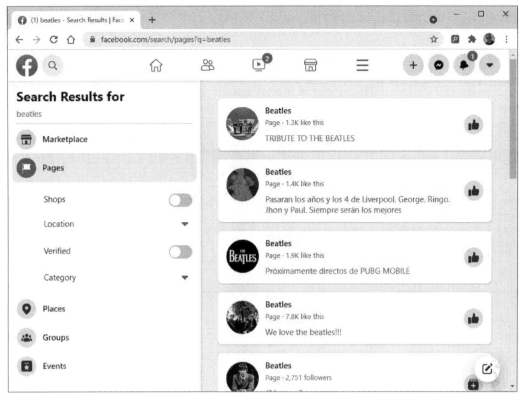

Figure 6.2

Then there are some other groups that people have made to discuss The Beatles that you can join if you wish to.

Figure 6.3 shows my Facebook home page, and, as you can see, there is a lot going on here, so it's easy to get overwhelmed if you are new to the site. But just because it's there doesn't mean you need to use it. If you just want to use Facebook to keep in touch with friends, then it's pretty easy to use and you can then ignore all the other features if you don't think you will want to use them.

The left hand column shows you all the types of areas that you can go to within Facebook such as finding friends, looking for groups, shopping, and so on. The right side of the page shows which of your friends are either online or have been online recently. If there is a green dot next to their name, then that means they are currently online (either on their computer or mobile device) and you can send them an instant message if you want to start up a conversation. Instant messages work sort of like text messages on your phone. If you have created any Facebook pages for things like groups or hobbies, they will show up at the top right under *Your Pages*. As you can see, I have a page shown for my computer help site Online Computer Tips.

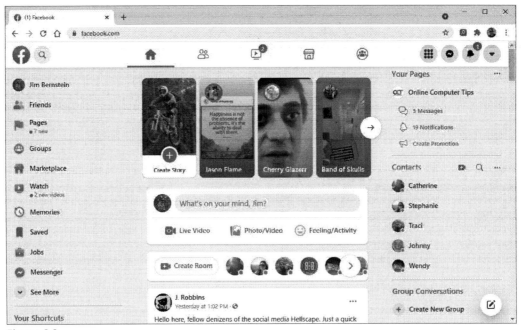

Figure 6.3

The middle of the page shows your feed, which will consist of posts from your friends and also other pages you follow (such as the one in my Beatles example). It will also display advertisements, so don't get confused if something shows up you don't recognize. You will also see things like suggested groups, friend requests, and so on.

At the top of the page, there is a section that says *What's on your mind* where you can create your own post that your friends can then read. You can even attach pictures if and videos if you like. You can also decide where you want your post to show and who can see it.

Figure 6.4

Also, at the top left of the page is a link with your name on it. Clicking on that will show you the posts you have recently made as well as other things such as your bio, friend information, likes, etc.

Speaking of who can see your posts and other information about you, I would take the time to go through some of the Facebook settings to make sure your privacy settings are the way you want them to be so only the people you *want* to see your information can see it.

If you click on the down arrow in the toolbar to the right, you will see the option for *Settings & Privacy* (this is also where you will go to logout). Once you are in the Facebook settings, you will see that there are many settings that you can configure, but I will be focusing on the ones that are geared more towards privacy and security.

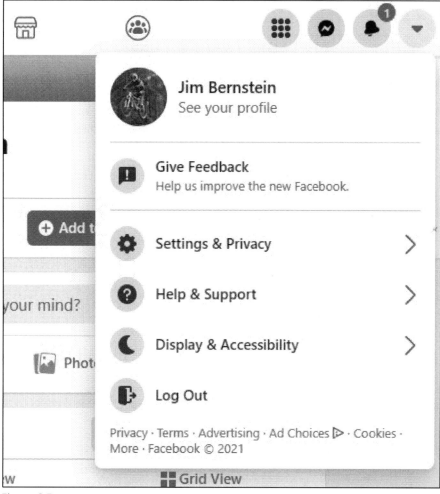

Figure 6.5

The first section I want to discuss is called *Security and Login* (figure 6.6), and it has settings for things such as how you log into Facebook and extra security options that you can enable.

The section labeled *Recommended* is where you can choose 3 to 5 friends that you trust to help you get back into your account if you forgot your password and have no idea what it could possibly be. What you would do is contact one of these friends, and they can use their Facebook account to contact them about helping you get back on to yours.

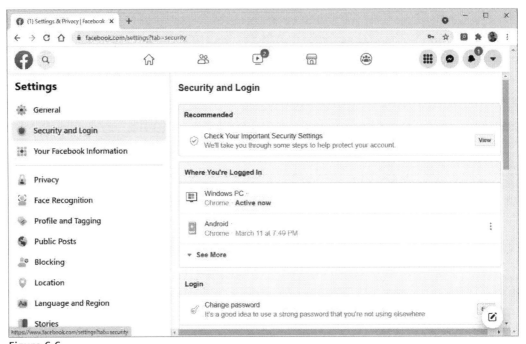

Figure 6.6

Next, we have the *Where You're Logged In* section, and this is used to show you where your account is logged in and on what type of device. So, if you think someone is getting into your account, you can go here and look for a location or device that you don't recognize and then take corrective action (such as changing your password).

Next, I would like to go over some of the settings in the *Privacy* section. Here you can tell Facebook who you want to see the posts that you make on your timeline. For example, if you click on *Edit* for the *Who can see your future posts* option, you will get choices similar to figure 6.8, which allows you the ability to fine-tune who can see your activity.

166

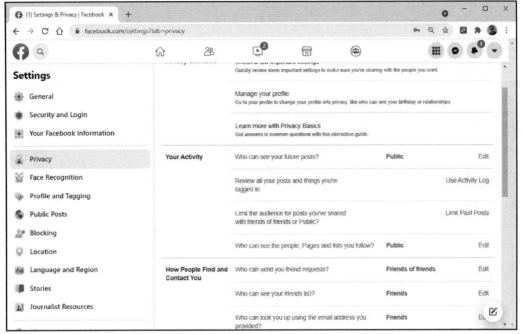

Figure 6.7

Figure 6.8

You can configure settings for similar things such as who can see your friends list, who can see your email address, who can see your phone number, and so on. I would definitely go through this section and adjust any of the options as needed.

Lastly, I would like to discuss the *Profile and Tagging* section (figure 6.9). This is another privacy setting that you can edit so others don't go posting things about you that you don't want to be posted. It's not foolproof, but it will help to adjust these settings.

The *Viewing and Sharing* options can be adjusted so you can decide who can post on your timeline. The options are your friends, or only you. At this time you can't pick and choose which friends can post on your timeline. The *Who can see what others post on your timeline* section *will* let you customize your choices though.

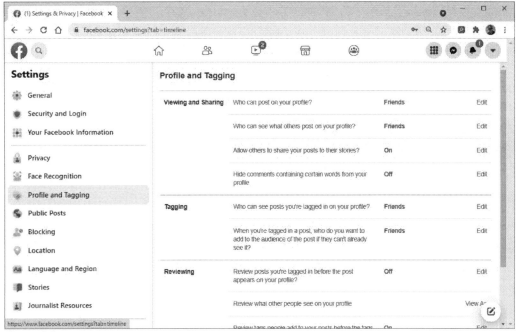

Figure 6.9

Tagging is when someone mentions you in one of their posts or adds a picture of you to their post. You can control who can do this with these options. So, if you don't want your name to appear in other people's posts without your permission, you should check out these options for sure.

As you can see from the images above, there are many other settings you can adjust to make Facebook work the way you want it to work. Just keep in mind that no matter how tight you lock things down, Facebook will always have access to your data, and you can't always trust them to do the right thing with it.

Instagram

If you are into sharing pictures of things like your pets, vacations, friends, or just about anything else, then Instagram might be for you, since that's pretty much what Instagram is used for. You can view your and other's Instagram accounts on your computer, but if you want to post to Instagram, you will need to do it on a mobile device such as your smartphone or tablet.

When you create an Instagram account you are the only one who will see your posts until you start acquiring followers, and then they will see your posts every time you upload a picture to your feed. So, if you make an account and want others to follow you, then you will need to notify them and tell them to look up your account name on Instagram to start following you.

You can follow others as well, and they don't even need to be people you know. Many people (such as celebrities or athletes) make their accounts public so anyone can follow them. If you don't want your account to be seen by anyone except people you want to see it, then you can make it private. Once you make your account private, people will have to send you a follow request to see your posts, your followers list, or your following list.

Figure 6.10 shows an example of a post from my mountain bike Instagram account when looking at it on a smartphone. It shows how many likes that particular post got, as well as any comments that my followers have left about that post.

Figure 6.10

Followers can click on the heart icon to like the post or click on the speech bubble icon to leave a comment. They can also share my posts with other people via things like email or text messages etc.

Figure 6.11 shows how my account looks on a web browser when using a personal computer. Notice how you can still do the same things such as like and comment on posts.

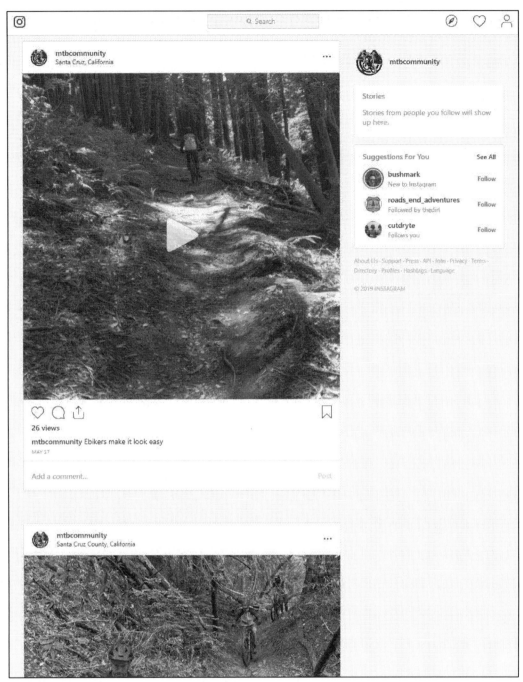

Figure 6.11

To create an account all you need to do is install the Instagram app on your device if it's not there already. Then sign up with a username, email address, and password. Since there are so many Instagram accounts already active, it might take you a bit to find a name that is not already in use.

Then all you need to do is click on the + button (which can be seen at the bottom of figure 6.10) and you will be asked where you want to get your photo (or video) from that you wish to post. You can choose from pictures you already have on your device, or you can take one on the spot to post.

Next, you will have the option to enhance your picture with a filter to change the way it looks (figure 6.12).

Figure 6.12

Then you can add some text describing the picture. In my example, I added *Fun times on the mountain*. Then you can add what they call a tag to your post. Tags are used to reference other people, companies, products, websites, and so on. You create a tag by adding the pound or hash sign (#) to the front of the word you are using for your tag. These are also referred to as hashtags. As you start typing in your hashtag (starting with the # symbol), Instagram will give you suggestions based on what you are typing. You can choose the one that matches or add your own if they don't have a suggestion for you (figure 6.13).

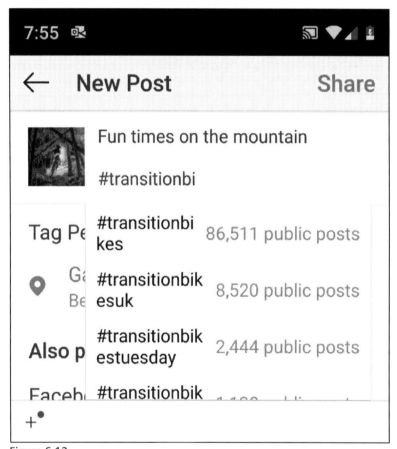

Figure 6.13

You can also add a location to your post so people know where the picture was taken. Instagram will give you suggestions based on your location by using the GPS on your phone. You can also manually type in a location. If your Instagram account is linked to your Facebook, Twitter, or Tumblr account, then you can have your picture automatically posted there as well.

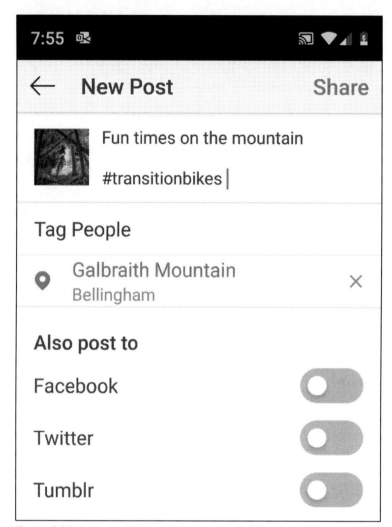

Figure 6.14

Once everything looks good, you will click on *Share*, and then your picture will be posted and show up in all of your follower's feeds on their accounts.

Twitter

Twitter is similar to Instagram except it's used more for posting comments or opinions rather than pictures (even though you can add those as well). You can use your mobile devices and computer to post to your Twitter account, as well as read other people's posts (which are called *Tweets*).

Just like with Facebook and Instagram, all you need to do is sign up for a free account and you will be ready to start posing. But, once again, you will need to get yourself some followers if you want anyone to read about what you have to say.

Figure 6.15 shows my computer support site Twitter account. On the top you can see that it says *What's happening* where I can type in a new Tweet to send out to my followers. I can also attach pictures and emojis and even create a poll that my followers can vote on.

Under that, you can see my latest post (Tweet) that has a link to a YouTube video.

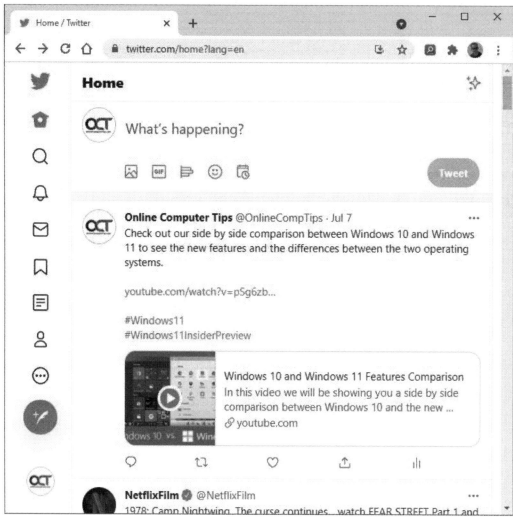

Figure 6.15

To create a new post, all I need to do is click on the Tweet button on the top right of the page and fill in the details about my tweet (figure 6.16). In my example, I am going to share a website link about an upcoming Gmail update. I am also going to include the Gmail icon image to enhance my post and make it stand out more. As of now, you can have a maximum of 280 characters per post. (By characters I mean letters, numbers, special characters, and so on.) When you add a website address like I did, it will count towards the character limit.

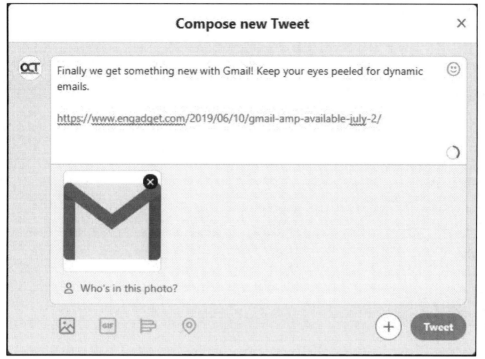

Figure 6.16

I then clicked on the *add image* button on the bottom left of the box and added the Gmail logo picture that I had saved on my computer. When you are ready to add your witty and profound comment, simply click on the *Tweet* button and it will be posted to your account and your followers will see it as well. Figure 6.17 shows my account after adding my new Tweet.

Figure 8.16

Of course there are more social media platforms besides Facebook, Instagram and Twitter so you might find yourself signing up for multiple accounts. Just make sure that you don't get so involved in these types of things that you spend your whole day online looking for likes and comments!

Chapter 7 – Using Email

After web browsing, what is the next most popular thing people do on the Internet? If you said sending emails, then you would be correct! If you don't already know what email is then you can think of it as sending a letter to someone but using your computer rather than an envelope and having it get there within seconds rather than within days. Email has been around almost as long as the Internet and many people actually have more than one email account.

To send an email you will first need to create an account with an email provider and then decide what method you will be using to send and receive emails. There are many free email services such as Google's Gmail, Microsoft's Outlook.com, Yahoo Mail, and so on that you can sign up for online. If you work for a business that has its own domain then you would be using a corporate email account. Many people prefer to use Gmail for their email address but I also like to use Outlook.com since it's easy to use and when you check your email online, the layout resembles the Outlook email client that many people are used to using on their computer.

Accessing Your Email

Once you get your account set up then you will need to determine how you want to access your email, with your main choices being using webmail or an email client on your computer. Webmail is when you go to the email provider's website (such as Gmail or Yahoo) to check your mail using a web browser. One benefit of using webmail includes being able to check your email from anywhere on any device that can connect to the Internet and has a web browser. Another benefit is that the email provider backs up your email for you, so you don't need to worry about losing anything if your computer crashes because it's not stored on your hard drive.

The other option is to use an email client such as Microsoft Outlook or Mozilla Thunderbird (figure 7.1). An email client is installed on your computer and then your email is downloaded to the email client and kept on your hard drive. Most email clients can configure multiple email accounts that can be used on one client, making it easy to stay organized. One downside to using a local email client is that you have to configure it to connect to the email server to get your messages. Fortunately, many newer clients will auto configure themselves after you enter your email address and password, but sometimes you will need to know things such as the incoming and outgoing server addresses and other techy type stuff.

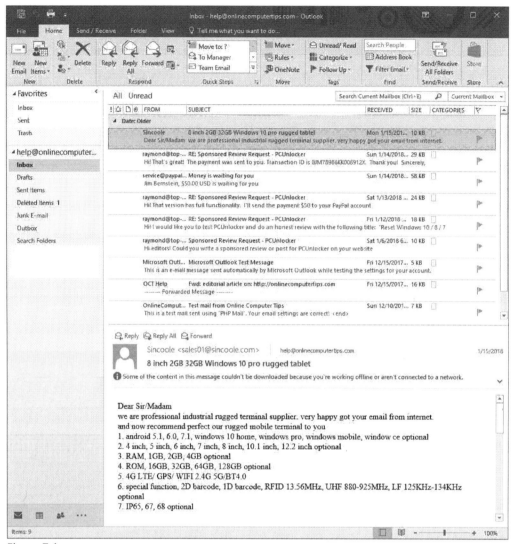

Figure 7.1

A benefit of using an email client is that if you lose your Internet connection, you can still look at any of your emails that were downloaded prior to losing the connection. These clients often have integrated calendars, which come in handy as well. Many online email providers have calendar options that you can also take advantage of.

Using Your Email Account

Now that you have your email account configured and are using either the webmail method or an email client installed on your computer, let's discuss the various components of email itself and how to use your account properly. There is much more you can do with your email account besides just sending and receiving basic emails. Like I mentioned earlier, many email clients have built-in calendars, and these calendars can be shared with corporate accounts as well as your email itself. All email clients have a way to store contact information (like an address book), so you don't have to try and remember their email address each time you want to send them an email.

Working with Emails

Once you get your email account set up and start sending and receiving emails, it's important to know how to work with your emails so you are sending them to the right people and keeping things confidential when they need to be. In this section, I will talk about composing a new email, replying to an email, forwarding an email, and, finally, blind copying an email.

Composing a new email consists of typing in the email address of the person or people you want to send it to or selecting them from your address book. To send to multiple people you can enter each email address on the *To* line separated by semicolons (most likely) depending on your email client. If you select the recipients from your address book it will put them in the To line automatically in the right format. A complete email address consists of the name, @ symbol, a period, and a .com or .net or whichever domain they are using. So **jsmith@microsoft** won't work, but **jsmith@microsoft.com** will work.

After you enter the recipient(s) then you can add the subject of the email in the subject line. This should be a brief description of what the email is about without too much detail, which should be saved for the body of the email. The body of the email is the area where you enter all of the information that you want to cover in the email. Here you can add a custom background to brighten up your emails, or a signature that summarizes who you are and your contact information, which can be automatically added to every email you compose. Once you have all the information the way you like it, then you can click on the *Send* button to send it on its way (figure 7.2).

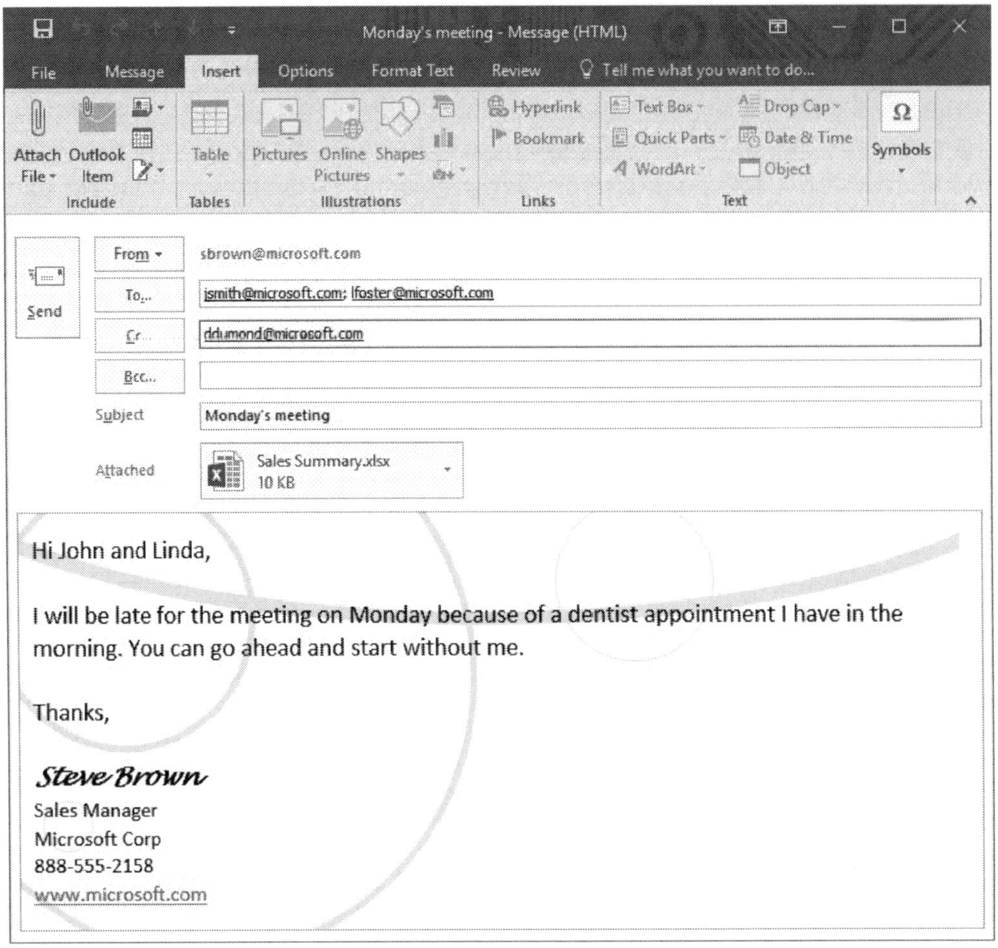

Figure 7.2

Sometimes you will receive emails and want to share them with other people, or they may contain information that someone else needs to know about. This is where forwarding comes into play. When you click on the *forward* button from within an email, you can then choose who you want to forward the email to. This will send an exact copy of the email to that person or people along with any attachments, but at the top of the message, there will be something added saying that it is a forwarded email from you. Also, a **FW:** will most likely be added to the subject line in front of the original subject noting that it's a forwarded email. You can usually edit out these changes, so it looks like the email was from you rather than one that you are forwarding from someone else. The forward button won't be available in new emails but only ones that have been sent to you.

When someone sends you an email that you want to reply to then it's just simply a matter of clicking the *reply* button, typing in your response, and then sending it on its way. You will usually see a reply option as well as a *reply to all* option. The reply option just sends the response to the original sender while the reply to all option will send your reply to everyone who was sent the original email. If you want to reply to all but one or some of the people on the email, then you can click on reply to all and remove the people you don't want to reply to from the list of recipients.

Finally, I want to go over a couple of special options you will see when composing a new email. They are the carbon copy (CC) option and the blind carbon copy (BCC) option. The carbon copy option is used to include another recipient or recipients in the email, but more for the purpose of just to let them know or as an FYI rather as showing that it is something that really concerns them or that they need to act on. The blind copy option does the same thing but the other people who receive the email won't see the BC email address as a recipient like they will other addresses from the To or Forward fields. This way you can include other people on the email without anyone else knowing they got the email.

Email Folders
Now I am going to talk about folders within your mailbox. Folders are used to organize your email just like you would organize files on your hard drive. There are default, or built-in, folders, and you can also make your own custom folders. The most commonly used default folder will be your *inbox* because this is where all new emails will arrive. Once you read an email it will stay in your inbox until you do something with it such as delete it or move it to a different folder. Emails that have not been read generally will appear in bold, and then once you read it the bold typestyle will be removed. There is an option to mark an email as unread which will make it bold again. You can do this if you want to keep an email as new for whatever reason you choose to do so.

Another commonly used default folder is the *sent items* folder. Every time you send out an email a copy will be kept in your sent folder so you can go back and review any emails you have sent out. This comes in very handy if you forgot if you sent an email or not and want to check, or if you need to see if you sent it to all the people you meant to send it to. Keep in mind that your sent items folder can get full quickly, so if you have a limit on how many emails your account can hold then you might want to clean out older sent items once in a while, especially if they have attachments, which can take up even more space. Many times you will have an option not to keep a copy of the email you sent in your sent items folder.

Finally, we have the default *outbox* folder, which is used to store emails that are ready to be sent out but have not been sent yet. The outbox is more common when you are using an email client on your computer rather than webmail. Many clients put the email in your outbox and then will send them out when you click on the *send\receive* button. Some people like this option because they can "send" a bunch of emails but keep them from leaving their computer until they are ready in case there are some changes that need to be made.

Within your webmail or email client, you will have the option to create your own folders. These are used to organize your email into whatever types of categories you desire. This is a good practice to get into because your inbox can get crowded very quickly if you get a lot of emails and this way you can make them easier to find if you categorize them. Of course, you can search your inbox as well as your folders, but keeping your inbox clean does make a difference. You can also make subfolders within your custom folders for another level of organization. For the most part, you can drag and drop emails from your inbox to another folder or from folder to folder.

Attachments
When sending emails, it's very common to want to include other items that the recipient may want or need. You can also send files along with your emails, and these are called attachments. Attachments can be almost any type of file, such as a document or picture. There are some files that you cannot send because they will most likely be blocked by the email server on the other end for security reasons.

To add an attachment to your email simply compose a new one or reply to an existing one and look for a button that says *add attachment*. In many email interfaces, it will be represented by a paperclip icon as you can see back in figure 7.2. After clicking on add attachment you will see the standard browse for files box. Then you just need to locate the file or files you want to attach and click OK. After, you should see your attached file(s) in the email that you are composing. If you change your mind, you can remove one or all of the attachments before sending the email.

Another thing to consider when attaching files to an email is the size of the attachment. Most email providers have size limits on received emails and sometimes even on outgoing emails. A typical size limit may be 10 or 20MB (megabytes), so if it too big you won't be able to send it via email. Most pictures are ok unless you are sending a large quantity in one email. For the most part, you can't email movie attachments because of their much larger size.

Pictures are one of the most commonly sent email attachments, and with a good camera or smartphone, your pictures can get quite large. Common sizes for pictures these days are 6-8MB *each*, so you can see how it would be hard to send a bunch of pictures in one email. If these are just pictures that people will be viewing on their computer and not something that you are sending out for artwork or printing purposes, then you should consider shrinking them down to make the file size smaller. This usually involves using some type of photo editing software, but there is a great (and free) utility called *Image Resizer for Windows* that you can download and use to resize pictures one at a time or in bulk to make them smaller while still keeping the image quality. Another way to include pictures in an email is to paste a copy into the body of the email rather than attach it. This method varies depending on the source of your picture. For example, if you found a picture on a website or in a document that you want to share, you can copy the picture by right clicking on it, choosing copy, and then paste it into the body of the email. This way the person on the other end can see the picture right in the message rather than having to download an attachment.

Sharing Website Links
Another common and very useful thing you can do with emails is to share website addresses. This way instead of trying to explain how to get to a certain website or page on that website, you can include a link right in the body of the email that the recipient can click on, and it will take them right to the page you are referring to. I discussed copying and pasting text back in Chapter 2.

To share a web page in an email all you need to do is to go to the page you want to share, highlight the address in the address bar, and then right click it and choose Copy. You can also use the Ctrl-C keyboard shortcut for copy. Then go to the email you are composing or start a new one. Right click in the body of the email where you want the link to go and choose Paste or use the Ctrl-V keyboard shortcut. You can add several links to one email, but just be sure to separate them by putting them on separate lines.

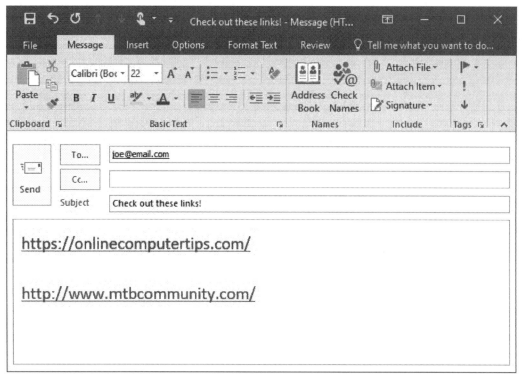

Figure 7.3

Chapter 8 – Printers

Printers have been around for as long as the personal computer itself, and if you have a PC in your home or office, there is a very good chance you have a printer as well. Printers are commonly used to print out documents, spreadsheets, photographs, and so on, and there are many options to choose from when selecting a printer to use with your computer. The prices of printers can vary quite a bit as well.

Types of Printers
There are many types of printers, and they each have their place in our homes and offices. There are also specialty printers as well, such as label printers, which have a more specific purpose. Many of these specialty printers you may never come across, and for this discussion I will be sticking with inkjet printers and laser printers since they are the most commonly used printers by far, with inkjet printers being the most popular for home users and laser printers being more commonly used in the office.

Inkjet Printer
Inkjet printers work by using tiny guns to fire tiny ink dots on the paper at precise locations to make up the text or image that you requested to be printed from your computer. They are fairly inexpensive, with the replacement ink being the biggest maintenance cost and sometimes even costing you more than the printer itself!

Some inkjet printers will have a single black ink cartridge and a single color cartridge, while others will have three separate color cartridges that you can replace as they run out of ink. There will be one for cyan, magenta, and yellow, and together they will create all the custom colors the printer is capable of putting on paper. As for the paper, inkjet printers require you have a lot of choices since almost any type of paper will work just fine. Most people use copy paper (called bond paper), and others will use inkjet specific paper, which is a little thicker. If the feeder on your printer will take cardstock, then you can even print on that. The only paper you might have trouble with is glossy paper unless your printer is designed to print photographs and has photo specific ink.

Print quality is very good these days, but not as good as it is in laser printers because of the way they work in comparison to inkjet. Depending on the model of the printer, you can get about 250 pages or so out of a single print cartridge (depending on what you are printing). You will know when you are running out of ink because the text or images will be lighter than they should be or will be missing sections completely. Or, when the page comes out blank that is a good sign you are out of ink, but, then again, it can also be a sign that your printer has died. Many inkjet printers have built-in monitors that work with the software to show you the ink levels in your cartridges.

Laser Printer
A laser printer differs from other types of printers (such as dot-matrix and inkjet) in the way that it doesn't directly put ink on the paper. It uses a laser along with electricity to fuse the image to the paper with toner. Here is how a laser printer works but it might be a bit of a TMI (too much information) discussion.

The core component of this system is the photoreceptor, which is a revolving, cylinder-shaped drum. This drum assembly is made of photoconductive material that is discharged by light photons. Before printing occurs, the drum must be cleaned to remove any traces of previous pages. The drum is given a positive charge by the corona wire, which is a wire with an electrical current running through it.

As the drum revolves, the printer shoots a small laser beam across the surface to discharge certain points to draw the letters and images to be printed as a pattern of electrical charges. The data in the printer's memory is written to the drum using this laser instead of ink or toner, and this process changes the electrical charge in those spots.

After the pattern is made, the printer coats the drum with a positively charged black powder called toner. As the paper is being drawn into the printer, the toner is applied to the drum. Since it has a positive charge, the toner clings to the negatively discharged areas of the drum, but not to the positively charged areas. At this point, the image is on the drum, along with the toner.

Finally, the printer passes the paper through the fuser, which is a pair of heated rollers. When the paper passes through these rollers, the loose toner powder melts and fuses with the fibers in the paper, making it stick to the paper.

The last step of the fusing process is the pressure roller. This is a rubber roller that presses against the fuser roller, and the paper feeds between it and the fuser roller. After putting the toner on the paper, the drum surface passes the discharge lamp. This light exposes the entire photoreceptor surface, erasing the original image and making it ready for the next print job.

Multifunction Printer

There are also multifunction (also called all-in-one) printers that can print, scan, copy, and fax all within one unit (figure 8.1). They tend to cost more than standalone printers, but these days you can get one for less than $200. They are larger than standalone printers, and usually require software to allow you to use all the features from your computer, otherwise you have to do it from the touchscreen on the printer itself, which can be cumbersome and not as customizable. HP (Hewlett Packard) is the king of these all-in-one printers and is one of, if not *the* top inkjet and laser printer manufacturers.

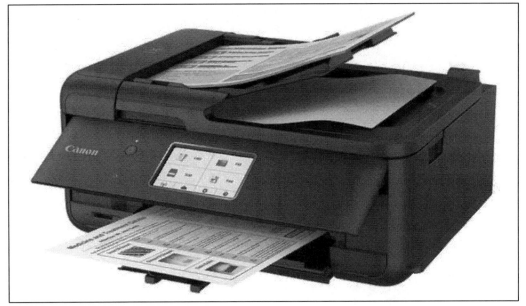

Figure 8.1

Printer Connections

There are several ways to connect your computer to your printer, and the method you use will depend on what your printer supports as well as the environment you are using it in. For home users, the most popular connection methods are USB and wireless, with wireless becoming the go to connection method these days. Most home use printers have more than one way to connect and may also offer a network connection in case you want to connect your printer to a network switch and share access to it that way.

Printers will usually only have one USB connection, so if you go with that method you will only be able to connect one computer to the printer. Of course, you can share the printer connection in Windows and others can print via or through your computer, but, then again, your computer will need to be turned on and accessible to the network. If you connect to your printer wirelessly then other computers can connect the same way, assuming they have wireless capabilities and not be dependent on your computer being powered on. You can also connect your smartphone to your printer wirelessly if the model is supported by your phone.

Figure 8.2 shows a typical USB connection between a computer and a printer.

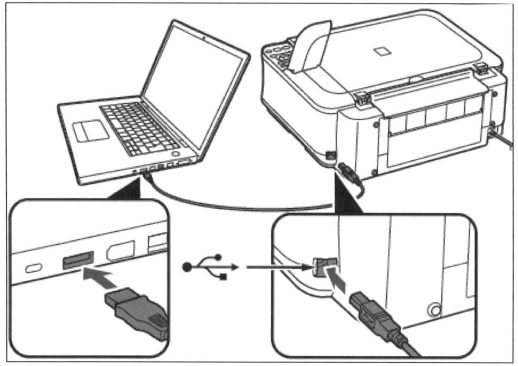

Figure 8.2

Installing Printers\Scanners

Printers are one of the most common devices that people add to their computers. These days most printers are what they call all-in-one printers, where they can print, scan, copy, and fax. And with these printers costing so little, they are affordable to just about everyone.

Most printers will install the same way no matter if it's an all-in-one printer, photo printer, or laser printer. There are a few different ways to connect them to your computer though, so let's talk about that first.

It used to be that using the USB connection was the most common way to connect a printer to a computer. Computers will typically have around 2-6 USB ports in the rear, and usually a couple in the front of the computer for easy access. The process involves connecting a USB cable from your computer to the printer and is as easy as that.

Another connection method that is becoming more popular than USB is to use a wireless connection. This method will probably be the standard way to connect soon, at least for home users. When you use a wireless connection, you can have multiple computers connect to one printer rather than being stuck with only one computer using the printer because there is only one USB port on the back of the printer. This method is a little more complicated to set up because you will need to connect your printer to your Wi-Fi router\modem first and then have your computer search for an available wireless printer to connect to.

Once you get the connection method figured out, you will need to install some software called a *driver* on your computer. Drivers allow the operating system (Windows) to communicate with the hardware device, in our case, the printer. Sometimes you will get lucky and Windows will already have a driver for your printer built-in and configure it for you. If not, then you will either have to use the software CD that came with the printer or download a driver from the manufacturer's website.

There is more than one way to install your printer software. If you install the software from the supplied CD, then it usually comes with the driver plus additional software for things like scanning and faxing. It's up to you which components you want to install, but you definitely need the driver. To install the driver and additional software from the CD, simply put it in the drive and it should automatically run. If not, then you need to use Windows\File Explorer to browse to the CD itself and find the setup file and run it from there.

Another way to install a printer is from the *Devices* section in the Windows 10 settings. Once you are there, you will click on *Printers & scanners*. There is an option to add a printer or scanner that you can click on (figure 8.3).

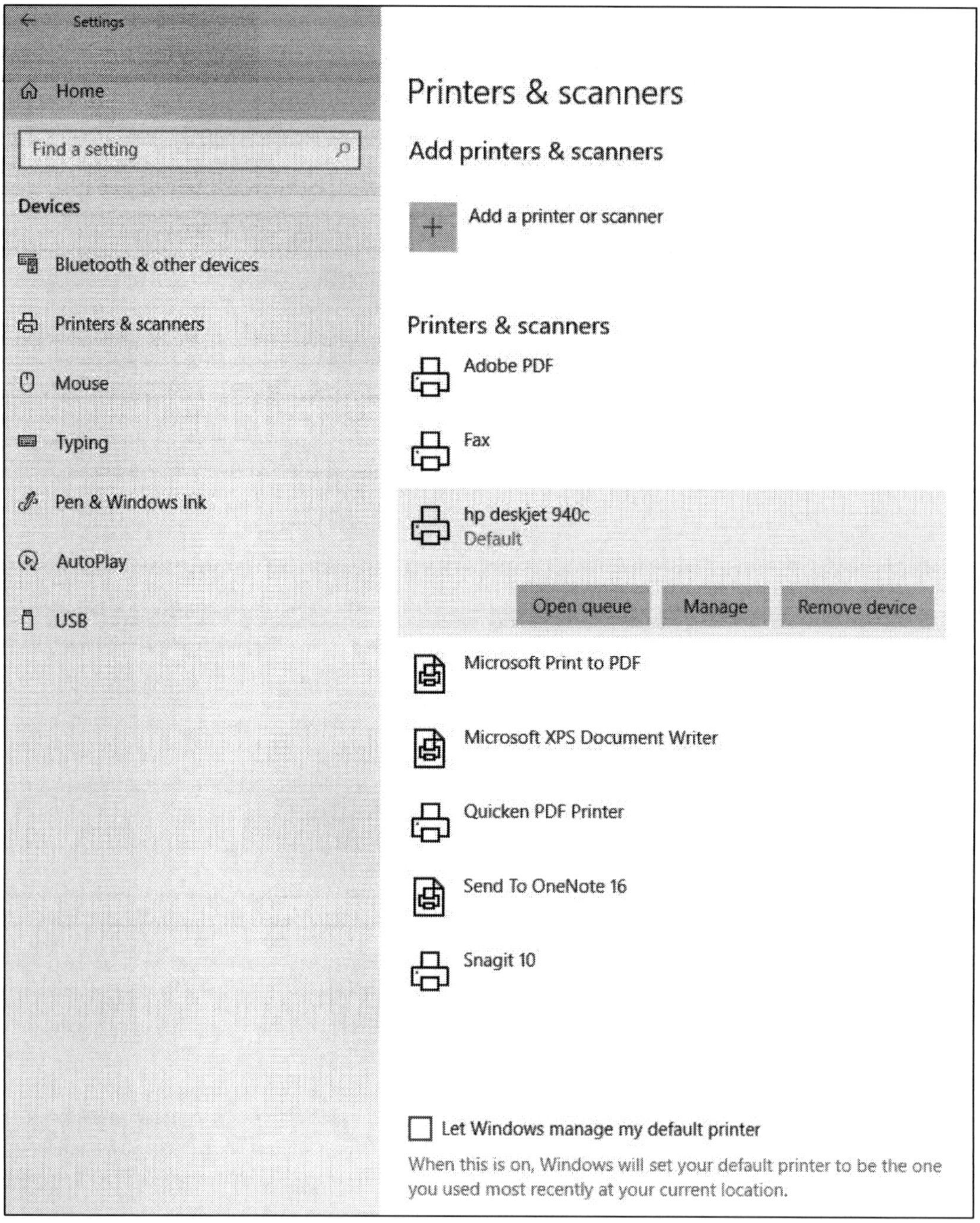

← Settings

⌂ Home

Find a setting 🔎

Devices

🖳 Bluetooth & other devices

🖨 Printers & scanners

🖱 Mouse

⌨ Typing

✒ Pen & Windows Ink

⟳ AutoPlay

🔋 USB

Printers & scanners

Add printers & scanners

➕ Add a printer or scanner

Printers & scanners

🖨 Adobe PDF

🖨 Fax

🖨 hp deskjet 940c
Default

Open queue   Manage   Remove device

🖨 Microsoft Print to PDF

🖨 Microsoft XPS Document Writer

🖨 Quicken PDF Printer

🖨 Send To OneNote 16

🖨 Snagit 10

☐ Let Windows manage my default printer

When this is on, Windows will set your default printer to be the one you used most recently at your current location.

Figure 8.3

Windows will then search for any new printers that are connected to your device. Once it finds your printer, it will prompt you for the location of the software drivers and then proceed to install the printer.

You might have noticed that in figure 8.3 there are some buttons next to the default printer that you can click on to do various things. The *Open queue* button will open the print queue for that printer and show you what jobs are being printed or are waiting to be printed. The *Manage* button will allow you to manage your printer's settings and properties. You can also run the printer troubleshooter from this section. Finally, the *Remove device* button will remove the printer from your computer.

Another place you can manage your printers from is called *Devices and printers*. It's the place you used to go for printer-related tasks in older versions of Windows, but is still included in Windows, and some people like it better. Just do a search for *Devices and printers* to find it.

Setting Your Default Printer

If you have more than one printer and have one that you use more than the rest, then you can set that one as your default printer. When you click on print within a program, it will automatically print to the printer that is selected as the default. If you want to print to a different printer, then you will manually need to change it before printing.

Changing the default printer is an easy thing to do. Simply do a search *for Devices and Printers* and once you are there (figure 8.4) simply right click the printer you want to set as default and then click on *Set as default printer*. If you know how to get to the Windows 10 Settings, click on the printer and then the *Manage* button and finally the *Set as default* button.

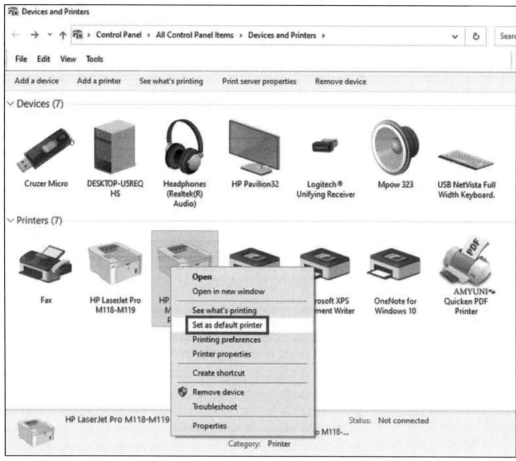

Figure 8.4

One thing to keep in mind when it comes to your default printer is that many programs will print to whatever printer was used last until you change it to a different printer again. For example, if you were in Word and changed the printer to a non-default printer to print your last document, then that non-default printer will be used for the next print job unless you set it back manually or close and reopen Word.

Printer Troubleshooting

Printers have their share of issues and tend to not work properly when you need them the most, but there are several things you can do to get your printer back online if you know what to look for. Printer issues can consist of things such as blank pages printing out, no pages printing out, strange characters on the page, and so on. You might require some assistance if it's not something simple like a paper jam or power cable issue. Here are some fixes you can try for certain types of printer issues:

Nothing printing at all
- Make sure the printer is turned on.
- Make sure the USB cable is connected if that method is being used.
- Check your wireless connection on your computer and printer if using a wireless connection.
- Click the printer queue icon by the clock in the Taskbar and see if there are any failed or backed-up jobs causing your print job not to go through. Clear out any backed-up jobs and try again.
- Look for error messages on your printer screen if it has one.
- See if your printer is listed as "offline" in Devices and Printers.
- Restart the Print Spooler service.
- Look in Device Manager for errors.
- Turn the printer off and on and maybe reboot the computer as well.
- Print to a different printer (if you have one) to see if the issue is computer or printer specific.

Printing blank pages
- Check the ink levels in the software if it's supported.
- Take the inkjet cartridge out and shake it to see if there appears to be ink in it.
- If you are printing something like black text, try changing it to red to see if it actually prints. (This way you will know it's your black ink cartridge that's causing the problem.)
- Install a new cartridge temporarily (if you have one) to see if it fixes the problem.
- Clean the print heads for inkjet printers using the printer software.
- Take the inkjet cartridges out and clean the tip where the ink comes out with a tissue.
- Take the laser printer toner cartridge out and shake it, then put it back in and try again.
- Make sure you are printing a page with something on it and not a blank page.

Paper jams
- Make sure the paper is properly aligned in the paper tray.
- Try a different paper tray or manual feed tray (if you have one).
- Make sure the paper is not curled or warped.
- Make sure you are not using paper not designed to run through your printer.

- Check the rollers for the paper trays and feeder for excessive wear or try cleaning them.
- Laser printers require periodic cleaning to function at their best.

Strange characters (gibberish) being printed on the page
- Check your printer property settings under the *Advanced* tab to make sure the right driver is being used.
- Download and install a new driver.
- If you recently installed a new driver or did some type of printer update, see if you can roll back to the old driver.

Chapter 9 – Office Productivity Software

If you have used a computer at work, then you have most likely used some type of office productivity software to create and edit things like documents and spreadsheets. This type of software has been around for about as long as Windows itself and keeps on improving with every new version. In fact, this type of software can do so many things that it can be difficult to master or to even really be able to take full advantage of all its capabilities.

Types of Office Productivity Software
There are many types of programs that are categorized as "for office use" but if you are just a home computer user or not a power user at the office you probably won't use most of the more complicated programs. Let's talk now about the most common types of programs that come with these office productivity programs.

Word Processors
One of the most commonly used programs in the office is the word processor. This type of program allows you to type up any kind of document you can dream of, from resumes to sales invoices. There are many software publishers that sell word processing software, from Microsoft with their Word product to Apache with their free Open Office suite. Most word processing programs have the same basic features such as formatting text, inserting pictures, and so on, but the more advanced ones will let you do things like add charts and graphs, comments, videos, tables, and even more. Figure 9.1 shows a Microsoft Word document with some of these advanced features in place.

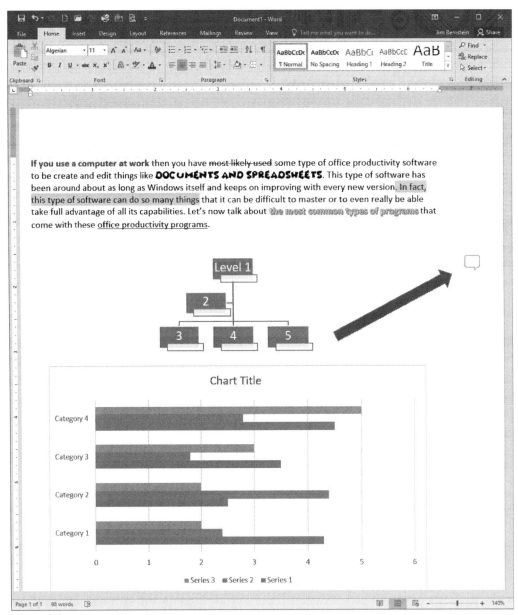

Figure 9.1

However, if you don't need all that fancy stuff and just want something to write some letters with, then you can even check out **WordPad** (which comes built in to Windows) and see if that works for you.

Spreadsheets

Spreadsheets are a more complicated tool than word processors and are used by people who need to store data in an organized format and be able to manipulate that data with formulas and other calculations. As you can see in figure 9.2, the

Microsoft Excel spreadsheet has a simple table with some header values, and then that table was turned into a chart and inserted into the spreadsheet itself. With spreadsheets, you can create formulas to manipulate data or use one of the built-in formulas. Many people just use spreadsheets as a place to enter basic data because it's easier to manipulate the columns and rows compared to trying to do the same thing with a word processing program.

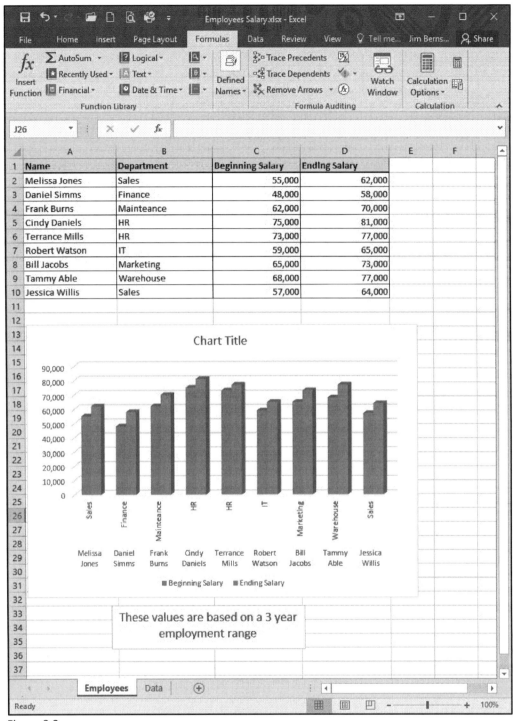

Figure 9.2

Presentation Software

If you have ever gone to a meeting at work where you had to sit through a presentation being shown from a projector onto the wall, then it was most likely created by some sort of presentation software. This type of software, for the most part, is fairly easy to use and involves putting text and pictures on slides and arranging them how you want them to be displayed during your presentation. You can add things like movies, music, and animations to spice them up a little and hope that it keeps people awake. Figure 9.3 shows a Microsoft PowerPoint presentation. On the left side of the screen are the slides with the main section displaying the current slide that is being worked on. You can add as many slides as you like and rearrange them as needed. Then, when you have everything looking the way you want, you can play it as a full screen slideshow on a projector.

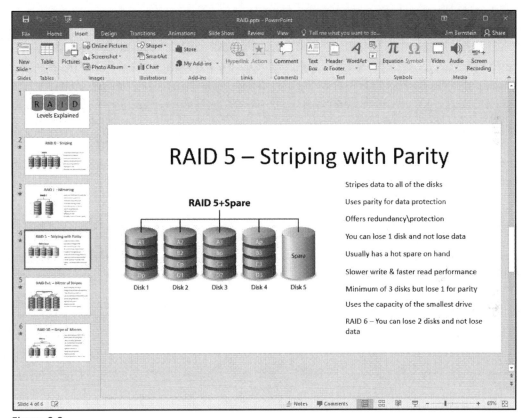

Figure 9.3

Microsoft Office Basics

Since Microsoft Office is the most commonly used office productivity software, I wanted to discuss how you would perform some of the basic tasks when using one of the Office programs since the tasks I will be going over also apply to most of the other Office programs. Microsoft calls their suite of programs Microsoft Office, and you can purchase it in various versions depending on which of the programs you need and your budget. If you were to buy the top of the line home version of the Office suite, it would come with the following programs and services:

- Word
- Excel
- PowerPoint
- OneNote
- Outlook
- Publisher
- Access
- OneDrive
- Skype

All of the Office programs use the Ribbon interface to house all of the tools you need to work with whatever program you are in (figure 9.4). The Ribbon was introduced in Office 2007 and replaced the standard text-based menus. The specific tabs on the Ribbon will vary a little depending on what Office program you are working on, but many of them are the same, such as the File, Home, and Insert tabs. The Quick Launch bar at the top left of the window is customizable, and you can add icons for items such as save, open, new, and print and have commonly used functions all in one place.

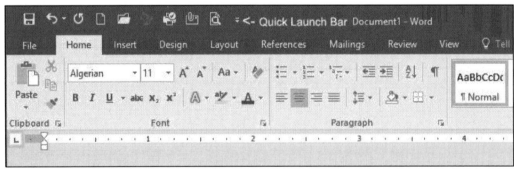

Figure 9.4

Opening, Saving and Creating Files
To open an existing file, you can go to the *File* tab, then either browse for a file to open or choose from a list of previously opened files. There are also options from the File tab to create a new blank file or open a predesigned template for things like resumes and reports. If you want to save or print a document, those options are under the File tab as well, but as you can see in figure 9.4, all of these options

are either on the Quick Launch Bar by default or have been easily added. The File tab works pretty much the same way for all of the Office programs.

Save vs. Save As

Speaking of saving documents, you need to know the difference between *Save* and *Save As*. Let's say you started a new document and did some work but haven't saved it yet. If you click on Save, you will be prompted to name the document and choose a location on your computer to save it. This will save it as a new file on your computer. Then the next time you click on *Save* the file will be updated with the latest and most current changes you have made to it. Now let's say you want to keep the currently saved version of the file as is but have made some changes and want to save them as a different file. This is where *Save As* comes into play because you are saving the file AS some other file rather than as the current file. So, after you click on Save As, name the file, and choose its location, you will have two different files, one with the old contents and one with the new changes and new name. One thing to remember is that you can't save a file with the same name as another file in the same folder, so if you choose Save As and pick a name of an existing file, then that existing file will be overwritten by the one you are saving.

Fonts and Font Sizes

Fonts are the typestyles you can use within your documents, spreadsheets, and presentations. They can be mixed and matched to spruce up the look of your documents or make them easier to read. You can only use the fonts that are installed on your computer, but it's possible to install many more fonts that you can download or buy.

To change the font for existing text simply highlight the text, go to the font dropdown menu under the *Home* tab, and choose the font you want to use. Or, if it's for new text, simply change the size before you start typing. With Office programs, Microsoft has added font previews for each one, so you don't have to guess as to what the font looks like. In figure 9.6 you can see the font dropdown list, which shows the font names in alphabetical order along with a preview of what each one looks like. At the top of the list, you will see the default theme fonts, as well as the recently used fonts.

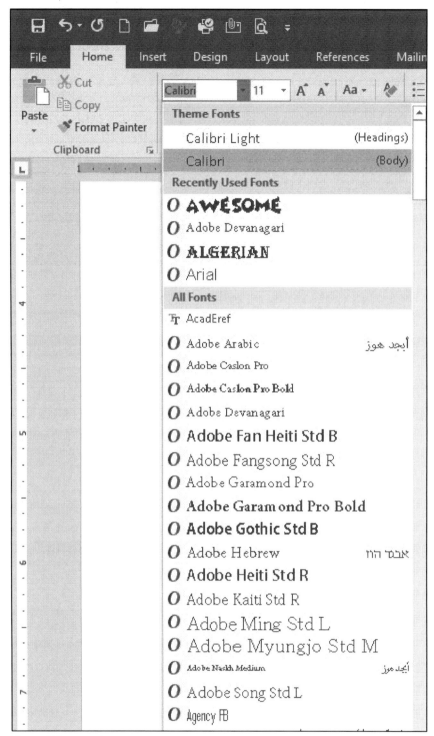

Figure 9.5

You will notice that there is a type size next to the font name. This controls how big the typestyle is on the page. Certain fonts will look bigger or smaller than others when used at the same font size, so it's always a good idea to try out different sizes to see what looks and fits the best.

Inserting Pictures and Other Objects

There is more to having a document that stands out besides just the text and some fancy fonts, especially for something like a presentation. This is where inserting items such as pictures, videos, shapes, charts, and so on will add some excitement to your work. Your choices for what you can insert will vary between Office programs, but if you go to the Insert tab you can see what types of things you can add.

To insert an object, you need to put the cursor where you want it or highlight the cell you want in Excel (etc.). Then, from the Insert menu, select the object you want to insert. Many objects that you can insert can be moved and resized after they have been placed. For some options, like inserting an online picture or YouTube video, you will have to specify its location or search for it.

Printing from Office Programs

I discussed printers in Chapter 8, so now I will focus on printing from Microsoft Office programs and what options you have when printing. If you don't have a print shortcut icon on your Quick Access toolbar, then you will need to go to the *File* tab and then click on *print*. From there you will have several options including the number of copies, what printer you want to use, what pages to print, paper size, and so on (figure 9.6).

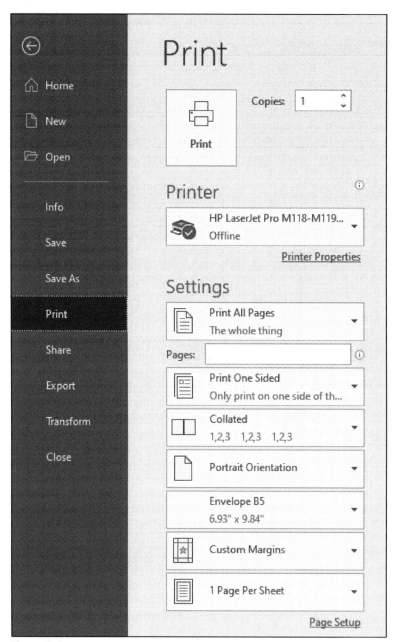

Figure 9.6

If you need to change any of the printer specific settings, you can click on the *Printer Properties* link and it will take you to settings such as changing the layout from portrait to landscape, changing the paper source and media type, as well as quality and color settings. Clicking on the *Page Setup* link will let you change things such as the document margins, paper size, and header and footer settings. If you decide that you don't want to print, simply click the back arrow on the top left to go back to where you left off.

As I mentioned before with Office programs, they will print to the last used printer if you don't change the printer from the File tab. So, if you change from your default printer to another one, print a page, and then click on print again, it will still print to your other printer and not your default. (Setting your default printer was discussed in Chapter 8.)

Emailing a Document from Within Office
Normally when you attach a document, spreadsheet, presentation, etc., to an email, you have to go to your email and create a new message and then use the add attachment feature. Within Office programs you can attach the file you are currently working on right to an email, assuming you are using an email client like Outlook and not webmail (which was discussed in Chapter 7).

To attach a document to an email from an Office program, go to the *File* tab and then to *Sharing*. Next, you will click on the *Email* icon and choose the type of attachment you want to use (figure 9.7). If you choose *Send as Attachment*, then the document will be attached in its current format, such as a Word document or Excel spreadsheet. If you want your document converted to a PDF file first so others can't easily edit it, then you would choose the *Send as PDF* option. The *Save as XPS* option is similar to the PDF option but is a Microsoft file type.

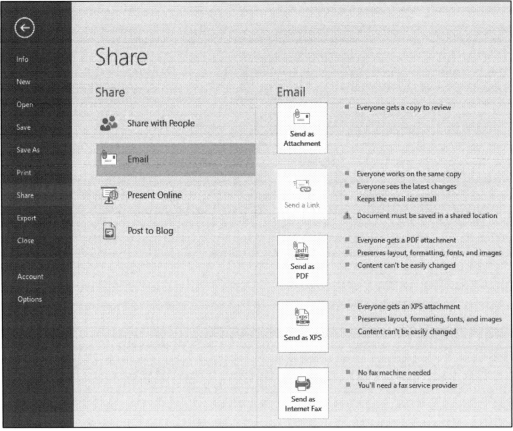

Figure 9.7

Chapter 10- Viruses and Spyware

Protecting your computer and your files from outside threats is becoming more and more of an issue these days, with the threats getting more serious and harder to fight off. Cybercriminals are coming up with more sophisticated ways to try and get valuable information from your computer, such as banking credentials and credit card information. Sometimes it's obvious when you have some sort of "infection" on your computer, and other times you won't even know until it's too late and they already got the information they wanted.

Viruses vs. Spyware

When you hear of the latest computer threat on the news or your favorite tech website, you might have noticed the terms "virus" and "spyware" used interchangeably. Even though this seems to be the norm, it doesn't mean that they are the same thing. There is a difference between the two, with spyware being the more popular type of infection people get these days, but both are still something you need to protect yourself against.

Viruses tend to be more destructive and are designed for a certain purpose, such as deleting your files on a specific date or slowing down all the computers to a crawl at your workplace. Spyware, on the other hand, is meant to steal personal and financial information and send it to its creator's computers so they can use it for illegal means.

How You Get Viruses and Spyware Infections

There are many ways to get a virus or spyware infection on your computer, and that's why it's always necessary to be careful and have the right type of protection, which I will be discussing next. One of the ways you can get viruses is from email attachments. These can be from people you know who didn't realize they were sending you an infected file from their computer, and also from junk or scam emails that have attachments that you have opened. Zip files and PDF files tend to be popular file types for transporting viruses. Word and Excel files can contain macro viruses that are designed to run within those programs, and then do anything from corrupting data to formatting your hard drive. So, the bottom line is to be careful when opening attachments and to make sure you know who the email is from and that the attachment was supposed to be there before opening it.

Another way to get a virus or spyware infection is by downloading software from the Internet. This is usually only a problem with free software since they try to entice you by making the software free so you will download and install it. There is a difference between free software and free software that offers a pay-for version as well. Usually when there is a free version and a pay-for version they want you to install the free version, then buy the one that costs money to get the additional features that the free one doesn't have. This type of software tends to be safer. So, when it comes to downloading software from the Internet, do your research, only download from reputable publishers, and try and read some reviews or do a web search to make sure it's safe.

If you have grandkids who like to play games online, then you need to check on the game sites that they are visiting, because many times they will have popup dialog boxes telling you that something needs to be installed to play the particular game and so on to get your child to click OK, and then it installs some type of spyware on your computer. It is common for other types of random popups to occur on these types of sites, and most kids click on OK to whatever pops up in front of them, so it's important that they know that it's not ok to just click OK to anything they see on the screen.

Another common way to get spyware on your computer is just by going to a website itself. When you get spyware this way it's called a "drive by download". Some of these malicious sites have ways of getting the spyware on your computer by visiting a site that takes advantage of a security flaw in your web browser or Windows itself. The most common sites that do this are illegal download sites, porn sites, and hacking sites. Any type of website that has some sort of shady content can be a place where you can get spyware put on your computer.

Available Software
There are many commercial as well as free antivirus and antispyware programs you can use to scan your computer for infections, as well as proactively prevent them from happening in the first place. Actually, many of the free ones work just as well, or even better than the pay-for kinds. The thing to be careful of is to go with a reputable software publisher because many free programs will actually do your computer harm after making you think it will help you by installing it. One common trick that is used is that you will install a free program, or you somehow get it installed without you knowing it, and it will tell you that your computer is infected with viruses. Then it will say the only way it can remove them is if you pay for the full version of the software when in fact there is no real infection on your computer at to begin with.

Some software will be virus specific while others will be spyware specific, and then there will be others that protect against both. The key to finding the right software for you is to do your research, check reviews, and talk with other people and see what they are using. You can check out our website and read reviews on this type of software as well.

www.onlinecomputertips.com/support-categories/virus
www.onlinecomputertips.com/support-categories/spyware

Manual Scans vs. Scheduled Scans vs. Real Time Protection
Like I mentioned before, you need to have effective antivirus and antispyware software installed on your computer to keep yourself protected from outside threats and cybercriminals. One thing you need to be aware of is that just because you installed some software, it doesn't necessarily mean you are protected. These programs don't always all work the same way when it comes to scanning your computer for threats. Some software requires you to run scans manually to check for issues, so if it's not something you remember to do, then the software is not doing you much good. Most software will let you schedule scans, at least in the pay-for versions, and many will automatically set up scheduled scans after you install it.

If you are able to use scheduled scans, be sure to check the settings to see if the software has set up a scan for you, or if you need to set it up yourself. Be sure to schedule the scan during a day and time where your computer will be on, otherwise it won't be able to run. You can schedule daily scans or for certain days of the week. Many programs will schedule daily scans, but that might be overkill unless you are doing things you shouldn't be doing on your computer on a regular basis. Once a week should be fine for most situations. Another thing to check for is any type of logging to make sure that the scan was run successfully and to see if any threats were found and how they were handled.

Besides manual scans and scheduled scans, many antivirus and antispyware programs offer real time protection. What this does is constantly monitors your computer's activity for malicious events such as when you download a file, open a file, go to a website, and so on. If it finds a potentially threatening situation it can block you from performing that certain action. If you decide that this is something you still want to do, then you can usually override the block and continue. The process for doing this varies between programs. Another feature that is often offered is email scanning, where the program will scan incoming emails and their attachments for threats. This is mostly for people who use email clients like Outlook on their computers.

Acting on Scan Results

Now that I have talked about the multiple ways that these antivirus and antispyware programs can scan and protect your computer, there leaves one more question: What do you do when the software finds a threat? There are usually settings you can adjust that determine what the software does when it finds threats, such as clean or delete infected files, remove the infection if possible, and quarantine files to keep them from causing your computer any additional harm.

What action you will take depends on what type of infection you have. For example, if you had a malicious file that was found in an email, you would delete it because you don't want that file causing any harm to your computer. If it's an important file on your computer that got infected, then you would want to clean the file to see if the infection can be removed so you can continue to use that file. Many times, it's not specific files that are infected, but rather Windows itself, and that's when you want to have your system cleaned so the virus or spyware is removed. When the software quarantines a file, it puts it in a locked area where it can't do any additional damage. You can then view these files and decide what action you want to take with them. This is the default for many antivirus and antispyware programs because you don't want them deciding which files get deleted and which don't. When your antivirus software finds an infection, you might want to give your computer expert family member or friend a call so they can help you clean things up.

Chapter 11 – Staying Safe and Secure Online

As discussed in Chapter 10, viruses and spyware are specially designed software created to harm your computer or steal your information, but some cybercriminals prefer to do their dirty work without the aid of software. Lately, there has been an increasing trend in more personalized computer scams, so in this chapter, I am going to talk about what to look out for and how to avoid becoming a victim.

Email Scams

Let's begin by talking about email scams since they seem to be the most popular type of scam these days and almost everyone uses email at home, at work, or both. One commonly used method by scammers is for them to spoof a name or an email address of someone you know so it looks like the email is coming from them, hoping you won't notice that it's not. Then they will include malicious files or links to sites that will attempt to steal your personal information or install some spyware on your computer.

If you ever get an email from someone you know, and it just has a link with no explanation or says something like "check this out!" then you need to be wary of it and check the email address to make sure it belongs to the person who sent it. Sometimes you can click on the name of the sender in the email to reveal the actual email address that was used to send the message. Another common practice is for cybercriminals to hack the passwords of real email accounts and use them to send out spam emails looking for someone to fall for their trick. Also, be sure to double-check links before clicking on them if you are unsure if they are safe or not. Many times, you can hover the mouse arrow over a link to find its real address in case it's been masked to look like something else.

Another thing they will do is send you emails that look like they are from your banking site and actually use the bank's logo etc. to make it look like the real thing. If you ever get one of these and they say there is a problem with your account or you need to do something like reset your password, call your bank rather than click on any links. And if the email includes any phone numbers for you to call, you can assume that they are not actually the numbers that belong to your bank but rather their own call center.

Figure 11.1 shows what looks like an email from amazon.com but if you look at the sender's email address it says *amazon@**support.com***. If this were real, it would say something like *support@amazon.com* so it's important to look at what comes after the @ symbol to make sure everything matches up.

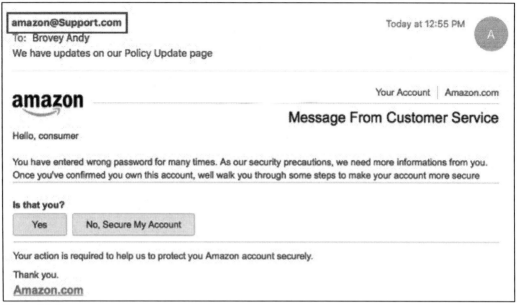

Figure 11.1

Phone Scams

Another tactic that is used to try and trick people into giving up personal information is the use of phone calls. What will happen is that these criminals will make calls and say that things like you owe the IRS or some bill collector money and if you don't pay they will be sending the authorities after you. Or they will claim to be from Microsoft or another similar company and say that your computer is infected with a virus or your copy of Windows is illegal and that you need to pay up to get things straightened out.

Sometimes they will try and convince you that they need to get on your computer to fix a problem that doesn't exist and will want to be paid for it. Then they will charge your credit card a couple of hundred dollars or so and have you give them remote access to your computer. Next, they will pretend to be fixing something while at the same time either stealing whatever information they can or planting some malicious software on your computer to do more harm after they are done. The bottom line is that nobody will ever call you to tell you that there is a problem with your computer because they have no way of knowing.

You should also look out for phone calls that have the same area code as you do. The scammers do this to trick you into thinking it's a local call or maybe someone you know but it is most likely coming from another part of the country or even a different country.

Website Popups

Popup ads are a way of life when it comes to surfing the Internet, so we either get used to them or employ some sort of popup blocker to keep them in check for us. The problem is that it's possible to get around these popup blockers or overpower them, if you will, with multiple pop-up ads.

Normally these ads are more of a nuisance than anything else, but the craftier ones can freeze up your computer with alarming sounds and scary messages, causing the uninformed to panic. Many times they will say things like your computer is infected and you need to click here or call this number to get it fixed. You will also see messages saying you are doing something illegal and your files will be deleted unless you call a specific number. If you call that number, you will then have to deal with the same scams I talked about in the last section on phone scams.

Figure 11.2

If this happens to you and you can't close out the ads, then try pressing *Ctrl-Alt-Delete* to bring up *Task Manager* to see if you can force your web browser closed by right clicking on it in the list and choosing *End Task*. If not, see if the Start button is working and try to shut down your computer, or at least save anything you need to save and close whatever programs you can before manually shutting down the computer by holding down the power button. Then restart your computer, see how things are looking, and run a manual virus and\or spyware scan.

It's never a good idea to simply turn off your computer without properly shutting it down because you risk file corruption and data loss that may make your computer not want to start back up again. This applies to computers running Windows as well as Macs.

Fake Antivirus Software

We tend to trust our antivirus software and assume that it is looking out for our best interests. With that in mind, another scam is to silently install fake antivirus software on your computer without you knowing it. This can happen when you go to non-trustworthy websites and many times the fake software gets installed in the background and then shows up later telling you that it found all kinds of infections on your computer. These are often called "drive by installations".

If you notice that there is some antivirus or antispyware software installed on your computer that you didn't install, then you can assume it's bogus and there to hurt you rather than help you. There are some exceptions such as when you install something like an Adobe Reader update and forget to uncheck the box that says it will install some free virus scanner along with the update. After this bogus software gets installed it will pop up notifications saying your computer is compromised and show you all the issues it found before asking you if you want them fixed.

The problem is that in order to fix them, you will need to buy the software first. Then after you do so it will "fix" the problems that never existed in the first place. If you see something like this on your computer, go to *Programs and Features* in Control Panel or *Apps* in the Windows settings and uninstall the software if possible or get some assistance from someone to help you. If it's not an option, then you will need to run your scanners to see if they can remove the software for you.

File Encryption Scams (Ransomware)

One of the worst kinds of threats currently out there involves getting a virus on your computer that encrypts all of your files and makes them inaccessible to you. When you encrypt a file, it takes that file and "scrambles it", for lack of a better term, so that nobody can read the file unless you have the encryption key to decrypt it. If you have any USB drives attached to your computer those files will most likely get encrypted as well. Plus, if you use a service like Dropbox there is a chance your remote files will become encrypted also.

This type of attack is often called ransomware because in order to get your files decrypted and put back to normal, you will have to pay a lot of money to get the key to decrypt them. This can often be $1000 or more. Even if you pay the ransom, there is still a chance you won't ever get the decryption key and just be out a lot of money. These attacks commonly come from different countries, so it's hard to prevent them or bring the criminals to justice. These types of attacks can come from something as simple as opening an infected PDF file from an email.

If you do get attacked by a ransomware virus then there is not much you can do except restore your files from a backup assuming you have one after you get your computer cleaned up. Your antivirus or antispyware software will most likely not be able to help you get your files unlocked.

Fake Websites

Another common way for cybercriminals to get your personal information is to create fake websites that copy legitimate websites in order to trick you into giving up your personal information such as passwords, credit card numbers, social security numbers, and so on.

They do this by duplicating an existing website, and many of them look so much like the real website that it's hard to tell the difference unless you know what you are looking for. Some things that will give away the fraudulent sites are spelling and grammar errors as well as low quality graphics and odd-looking text.

The way to distinguish the real site from the fake site is by its URL (address). Many times these sites will have a similar address, but just be off by one letter hoping you won't be looking or notice the difference. For example, if your banking site address is **http://www.safebank.com**, then they might make a fake site with an address of **http://saferbank.com** and count on you not noticing the difference. Then they would send you a fake or spoofed email with a link to the fake site saying something like there is a problem with your account and hope that you go there and log in, which will give them your name and password to the real site that they can use for their own evil purposes. Thankfully, you can't have two websites with the exact same address, otherwise we would all be in a load of trouble!

Secure vs. Unsecure Websites
By now you should have realized that the Internet is not a 100% safe place to be and that there are risks involved when going online. Thankfully, there are some methods that are used to help keep you safe when surfing the Internet. One of these methods involves securing websites in order to assure you that you are going to the site you want to be going to. To make a website secure, the administrator needs to purchase a security certificate from a trusted certificate authority and install it on the website to prove that they are who they say they are, and that all information passed back and forth between your computer or device and the website is over a secure connection. Most modern web browsers will let you know when your connection is secure or unsecure, but still let you access the site either way.

Just because a website is not secure doesn't mean that it can't be trusted and that you should avoid going to it. Many websites don't have any need to be secured because they are just for informational purposes and there is no need for you to input any personal information while on that site.

You might have noticed that website addresses begin with http even though many browsers hide the http and even the www in the address bar. When a site begins with http, that means it's not secure, and your browser should display a warning like the one seen in figure 11.3 (which is actually my mountain bike website).

Figure 11.3

On my computer website, I do have a certificate installed, and many websites are going with certificates even if they really don't need them just so they can assure you of their security. Notice in figure 11.4 that the address begins with https, and the S at the end stands for secure. There is also a lock icon next to the address indicating that it's a secure website.

Figure 11.4

Not all web browsers will show secure and unsecure websites the same, but it should be easy to figure out if the site is secure or not. For example, figures 11.5

and 11.6 show two other browsers, and you can see how they both use the same lock icon to indicate a secure website.

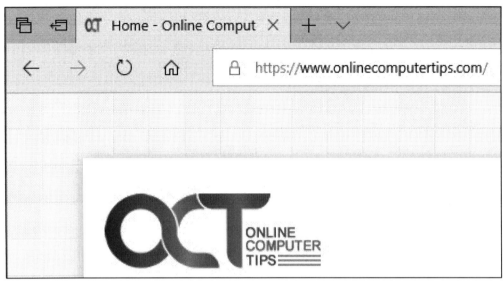

Figure 11.5

Figure 11.6

If you are going to a website where you will be logging in with a username and password or entering any kind of personal information into a form, then you need to make sure that it is a secure website, otherwise you risk getting your information stolen. If it's a banking website or shopping website, then you *really* need to make sure that it is secure otherwise you are asking for trouble. Any banking or shopping website that is not secure should not be up and running, and might even be a fake site to begin with.

If you get to your commonly accessed websites from your bookmarks, then you should be okay because they don't change unless you manually change them. (Just be sure your bookmark addresses are correct to begin with!) But if you do a search for a website such as your banking site, then make sure the link you are clicking on from the search results is the right one.

Figure 11.7 shows the results I get when searching for *Peoples Bank*. As you can see, there are several results, and they all have different addresses, so it's important to know the right address of the site you are trying to go to when it has to do with security, or a site where you might have to enter your personal information.

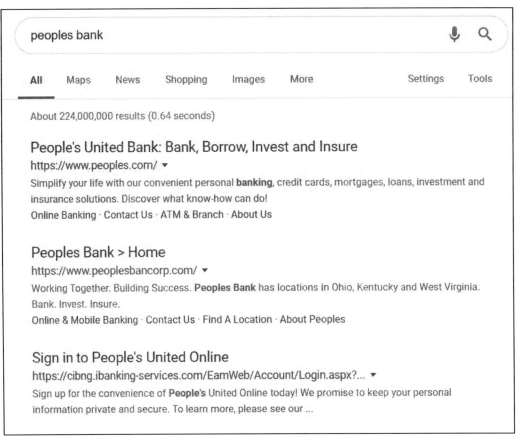

Figure 11.7

If you look closely at all the search results in figure 11.7, you will see that all the addresses start with https, meaning they are secure websites, which is critical for banking sites to be. Try and get in the habit of noticing this in your search results for your own safety.

This also applies when people email or text website addresses to you. Before you click or tap on the link, give it a once over to make sure that everything looks okay so you can have an idea of what website it will be taking you to rather than just blindly clicking and hoping for the best.

Providing Personal Information

When you do things like shop or bank online, you are expected to provide certain types of information such as your address, phone number, account number, and so on. But this doesn't mean you should just give any site the information they ask for. If you are on a site that does not require you to give out any information, then there is really no reason to do so. For example, you might go to a website and it will give you a popup to sign up for its mailing list. If you don't plan on using this site again or want to get emails from them, then don't feel obligated to provide them with your email address.

Many times you will go to a website such as a shopping site and it will want to know your location to show you their local stores, or maybe estimate shipping costs. When this happens, you may get a popup similar to what is shown in figure 11.8.

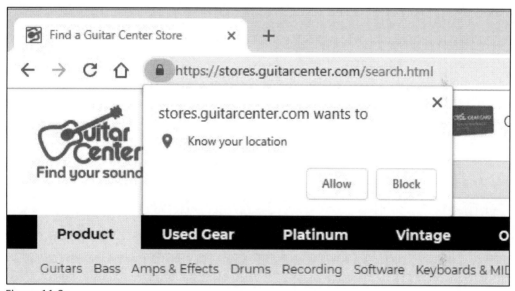

Figure 11.8

If you are okay with providing the site with your location, then you can click on *Allow* and it will tailor its results based on where you are. For the most part, there is no harm in doing this, but if you really don't have a need to give them your location, you might as well click on *Block*.

When shopping online you will often get asked if you want to save information such as your shipping address or credit card number. This is completely up to you because that way you won't need to type in the information each time you buy something from that site. I'm usually okay with saving my address on sites that I use often, but for the most part I don't let them keep my credit card information. (I do make one exception for Amazon.com because of how often I use their site.)

 You should **never** give out your social security number unless you are absolutely sure the site is secure and it's actually a site that requires it. When typing it in you should see that what you are typing is hidden as you type. If it's not, then that might be an indication that you shouldn't be entering it in there.

Saving Your Login Information

Since technology has made our lives easier, it has unfortunately made us lazier as well. Nobody likes to type in their username and password every time they go to a website or have to remember what password they even use for that site. All web browsers offer the ability to remember login information for specific websites so that when you go to that website, the information is already filled in for you or, better yet, it just logs you in automatically.

For many sites this is okay as long as it's a website that won't cause you any personal or financial problems if someone was to get your login information. But for things such as banking, tax, or medical websites, you should *never* let your web browser save your login information because if someone gets into your computer, they will be able to get your saved names and passwords and will be able to use them to log into things such as your bank accounts, etc.

Figure 11.9 shows some of the saved passwords kept in the Google Chrome web browser. All you need to know to view any of these passwords is the password for the computer itself, so you can see how easy it would be to have all of your usernames and passwords compromised.

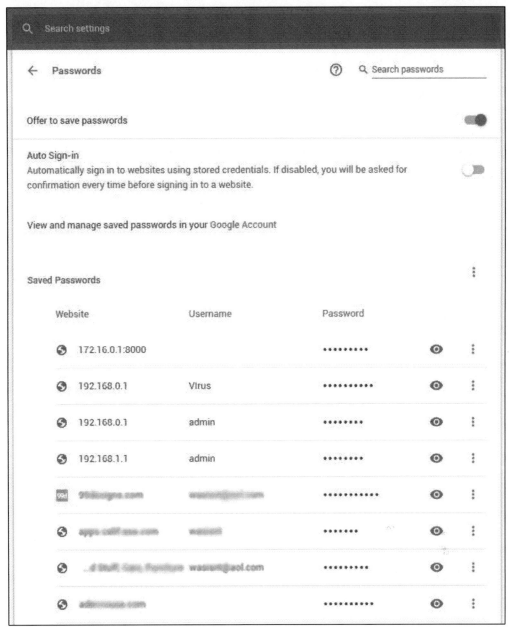

Figure 11.9

If you look closely, you can see the options to turn off the offer to save passwords feature, and also the automatic sign-in feature. These settings will vary from browser to browser and device to device.

If you have a saved login that you want to get rid of, you should be able to just remove the saved information for that site rather than have to remove all of them or disable the ability for your web browser to save logins\passwords altogether. (How you do this will vary on your browser and device, of course.)

Browser Toolbars

Browser toolbars are another one of those things that can be legitimate, or caused by malicious software getting installed on your computer. Toolbars are add-ons to browsers that add additional functionality such as buttons to easily check your email, the weather, or do specific types of searches. Not all toolbars are bad, and some people actually install them on purpose.

Figure 11.10 shows some examples of toolbars that can get installed within your web browser. Many times when this happens you will notice that your homepage also gets changed to match the toolbar that got installed. For example, let's say your homepage was Bing.com and all of a sudden you noticed you had a toolbar called *Social Search* and now your homepage was changed to *Social Search* as well. (FYI, your homepage is the website that loads when you first open your web browser and also what gets loaded when you click the home button in your browser.)

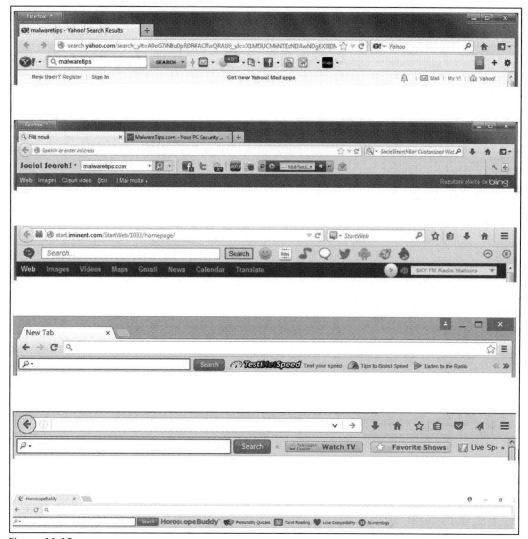

Figure 11.10

Many times all you need to do to get rid of these toolbars is uninstall them from your computer the same way you would uninstall any other type of software. (You may also have to use antispyware software to get rid of them if that doesn't work.) You might also be able to remove them from your browser add-ons, which is a little more advanced procedure.

Chapter 12 - Protecting Your Computer

When it comes to keeping your data safe, there is more to the story than just keeping your files and your personal information safe. You will also need to protect your actual computer itself from things like power surges, the elements, and other people. In this chapter, I will talk about things you can do to keep your computer safe, which in turn will help keep your data safe.

Surge Protectors

The purpose of surge protectors is to protect electrical devices from voltage spikes. They do this by limiting the voltage supplied to an electronic device by either blocking or shorting to ground any unwanted voltages above a safe threshold. They come in a variety of shapes and sizes, as you can see in figure 12.1, and these different models provide various levels of protection.

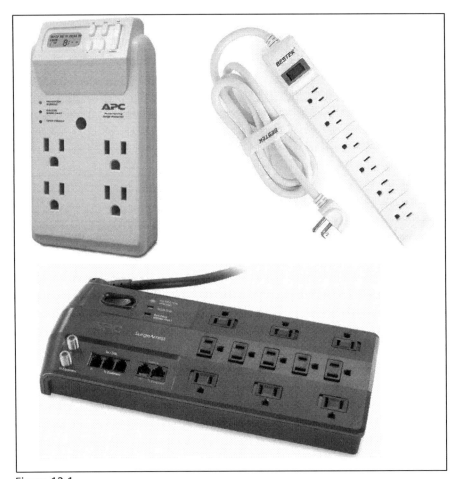

Figure 12.1

UPS

A UPS, or uninterruptible power supply, is a device that is used to power devices such as your computer and monitor that are plugged into it for a short period of time when the power to your home or office goes out. They can do this because they contain a battery or batteries that keep your devices running when the power goes off. They can switch to battery power instantly, so your devices won't even know they are now running on battery power. Then you can shut down your computer properly before the battery time of the UPS runs out. The UPS is plugged into the wall, and then your computer etc. is plugged into the built-in outlets on the UPS (figure 12.2).

Figure 13.7

They come in various "sizes" that will let you run a given number of devices for a given amount of time. So, the more devices you have connected to your UPS, the less time they will stay running when the power goes out because it's more of a drain on the battery. When purchasing a UPS you should see what kind of uptime they offer based on how many things you have plugged into them. Also consider how many devices you will be plugging into it, and what their power usage is. Then you can determine how much battery time you can get for all of your equipment when the power goes out.

Cooling
Keeping your computer cool is essential in its longevity and also its performance. When a computer runs hot, you risk the chance of damaging components such as the processor and motherboard. When some components get too hot they will simply stop working and become useless, even if you get things cooled off again. Also, when things get too hot you may notice that Windows will start acting up and freezing or crashing.

Computers have multiple fans located in various places such as inside the case, in the power supply, and on the processor. If one of these fans goes bad or begins to spin slower than what is required to keep things cool, then you will start having problems. Many computers will shut themselves off when heat levels get to a certain point, which is better than frying components, but you might then be looking at data loss and file corruption because of improper shutdowns.

Where you keep your computer will also affect its cooling. If you leave it on all day upstairs in a hot climate with no air conditioning while you are at work, then it may be too hot of an environment for the computer to be able to keep itself cool. Doing things like placing your computer under your desk with no ventilation can also be a potential overheating problem. You will notice that your computer case has vent holes for cooling, so if they get blocked, then the hot air has no way to escape.

Theft
Another thing you need to be concerned about when it comes to protecting your computer is theft by other people. This might not be too big of an issue in a secured office building, but it can be a concern with your desktop at home. All it takes is for someone to walk through an open door and snatch your computer, take it home, and then proceed to get all of your personal information off of it.

Laptops are especially vulnerable because you often take them with you outside of your home, and they are much easier to grab and carry away when you are not looking. Many people use their laptops at coffee shops etc., and all it takes is a quick bathroom break to give someone the opportunity to steal it.

For the home user, there isn't much you can do except to treat your computer like any other valuable possession such as your TV or your jewelry and be conscious of its location and who has access to it. Businesses usually have their important servers with user files stored on them locked up in server rooms that require special access to get into.

Cleaning Your Computer

Just like anything else in your house, your computer can become dirty just from sitting around in the same location, and at some point you are going to need to give it a cleaning. By cleaning I don't mean spraying disinfectant on it and giving it a rinse in the sink. You should always be careful when cleaning your computer and take the appropriate steps to do it right.

Dust Problems

It seems that computers love to collect dust inside and outside of their cases, and it's something that needs to be cleaned off periodically otherwise you are looking at some potential trouble. Dust on the outside of the computer is not too big of a deal and can be removed the same way you remove it from your furniture. But dust on the inside of the computer can cause overheating problems and also affect how the fans inside the case are working.

To clean the inside of the computer you will need to first shut it off and unplug it from the wall. Then carefully take off the cover so you can see the components inside. Take a can of compressed air and blow all the dust off the inside of the computer, the fans, and also the power supply fan from the rear of the power supply itself. If the compressed air can gets too cold and starts spraying out liquid, then stop and come back to it later. Never wipe things down with a rag or use a vacuum cleaner because you don't want to bend or break off any resistors or diodes etc. Also, make sure to blow out the vent holes on the cover as well to allow for proper airflow.

Cleaning Your Monitor

Just like with your smartphone, tablet, and TV, your monitor will get dirty and possibly full of fingerprints or other smudges over time and will need to be cleaned. Once again, you don't want to spray it with cleaner and hose it off, and you should try to be a little careful when cleaning it.

To begin with, give it a good dusting like you do with your TV and furniture to get the dust off of it. Then get a clean, soft towel and get it a little bit damp. Next, wipe down the monitor with the wet part of the towel to remove any smudges or fingerprints. Finally, use a dry part of the towel or a new towel to dry things off and give it a nice shine. Be careful not to put too much pressure on the screen when cleaning it to avoid damage. You might have seen monitor specific cleaning spray, but it's really not necessary to use.

Cleaning Your Mouse and Keyboard
The dirtiest part of anyone's computer is usually the mouse and keyboard since they get the most abuse from dirty hands and food and drinks being spilled on them. It's a good idea to give them a good cleaning once in a while for the sake of appearances and to clean who knows what out of them.

For the keyboard, you can use the same compressed air that you used for cleaning the dust out of the inside of the computer. This way you can blow all the dust and crumbs out from in between the keys that you normally wouldn't be able to get to. Then, with the computer off, you can use a damp towel again and give the keys a wiping down. You don't want to do this with the computer on because you might press some key combination you don't mean to and cause something you don't want to happen on your computer.

For the mouse, you can give the crevices a blowing out with the compressed air as well, then take a damp towel and clean off the smudged on grime from the mouse keys and mouse wheel. Back in the old days of mouse balls (before laser mice), you would have to take out the ball and clean all of the dust off of it as well. Once again, do this with the computer off so you don't click on something you shouldn't.

What's Next?

Now that you have read through this book and learned how Zoom works and what you can do with the software, you might be wondering what you should do next. Well, that depends on where you want to go. Are you happy with what you have learned, or do you want to further your knowledge of Zoom and online meetings or even take the next step and learn about other online meeting platforms such as GoToMeeting?

If you do want to expand your knowledge and computers in general, then you can look for some more advanced books on basic computers or focus on a specific technology such as Windows or Microsoft Office, if that's the path you choose to follow. Focus on mastering the basics, and then apply what you have learned when going to more advanced material.

There are many great video resources as well, such as Pluralsight or CBT Nuggets, which offer online subscriptions to training videos of every type imaginable. YouTube is also a great source for instructional videos if you know what to search for.

If you are content in being a proficient Zoom user that knows more than your friends, then just keep on practicing what you have learned. Don't be afraid to poke around with some of the settings and tools that you normally don't use and see if you can figure out what they do without having to research it since learning by doing is the most effective method to gain new skills.

Thanks for reading **Computers for Seniors Made Easy**. You can also check out the other books in the Made Easy series for additional computer related information and training. You can get more information on my other books on my Computers Made Easy Book Series website.

https://www.madeeasybookseries.com/

You should also check out my computer tips website, as well as follow it on Facebook to find more information on all kinds of computer topics.

www.onlinecomputertips.com
https://www.facebook.com/OnlineComputerTips/

About the Author

James Bernstein has been working with various companies in the IT field since 2000, managing technologies such as SAN and NAS storage, VMware, backups, Windows Servers, Active Directory, DNS, DHCP, Networking, Microsoft Office, Photoshop, Premiere, Exchange, and more.

He has obtained certifications from Microsoft, VMware, CompTIA, ShoreTel, and SNIA, and continues to strive to learn new technologies to further his knowledge on a variety of subjects.

He is also the founder of the website onlinecomputertips.com, which offers its readers valuable information on topics such as Windows, networking, hardware, software, and troubleshooting. James writes much of the content himself and adds new content on a regular basis. The site was started in 2005 and is still going strong today.

Made in the USA
Coppell, TX
19 October 2021